Fire Beneath the Frost

BY PEGGY BILLINGS

DEDICATION

This book is dedicated to the people of Korea. The title aims to show that their spirit will survive in spite of adversity. The fire burns no matter how thick the frost of winter.

Fire Beneath the Frost

by
PEGGY BILLINGS

WITH
MOON, TONG—HWAN
HAN, WAN—SANG
SON, MYONG—GUL
PHARIS HARVEY

Friendship Press, New York

Library of Congress Cataloging In Publication Data

Billings, Peggy.
Fire Beneath the frost.

Bibliography.

1. Protestant churches—Korea-History.   2. Korea—Civilization—Miscellanea.
I. Title.

BR1325.B54   1983   280'.4'09519   83-16525

ISBN 0-377-00135-X

Unless otherwise stated, all Bible quotations used in this book are from the Revised Standard Version, Copyright 1946 and 1952, by the Division of Christian Education of the National Council of Churches of Christ in the United States of America. Such quotes have been edited for inclusive language concerns according to that organization's guidelines.

ISBNO-377-00135-X

Editorial Office: 475 Riverside Drive, Room 772, New York, N.Y. 10115
Distribution Office: P.O. Box 37844, Cincinnati, OH 45237
Copyright © 1984 Friendship Press, Inc.
Printed in the United States of America

ERRATA

FIRE BENEATH THE FROST

Certain changes were made in the text of this book that are not reflected in the Study Action Guide. To integrate the text and the Guide, therefore, please note the following:

p. 85, Column 2, Session One:

> The chapter title is now "The People of Han."
> Item 5: The poem by Kim, Chi Ha is on p. 3.

p. 85, Session Two:

"Korea and the Powers: The Hare in the Tiger's Den."

> This chapter is now Chapter IV, so references on p. 86 to Chapter II
> should read Chapter IV.

p. 86, Session Three:

"The Role of Major Religions."

> The essential material for this session is in Chapter V, "Major Religions,"
> hence references in Session Three to Chapter III should be changed to
> Chapter V.

p. 87, Session Four:

> "Christianity in Korea" relates to material in Chapter II and Chapter III.

p. 87, Session Four, line 4 — the first word is *influenced*.

p. 87, Column 2:

> Subgroup D Assignment relates to Chapter III (not Chapter IV).

p. 87, Session Five:

> "From 'Han' (Suffering) to Joy."
> Basic material for this session is Chapter VI rather than Chapter III.
> Therefore change the mention of Chapter III under "Preparation"
> to Chapter VI. Please note also additional material on pp. 46-47
> and pp. 75-77.

p. 88, line 9 — read *are* for *ar*.

INTRODUCTION

The year 1984 marks the 100th anniversary of Protestant witness in Korea, a significant event for Korean and North American Christians. The Centennial offers Korean church members the opportunity to reflect on a period of growth that has been unique in Asia. United States and Canadian citizens can learn from Korea's mission activity and church development.

For the past 100 years, the Korean peninsula has been a stage for China, Japan, Russia and the United States to act out their dramas of vested interests. In this study, we will examine the web of cultural, social, political, economic and geographic realities and relationships of the last 100 years. This web forms a pattern rich in texture.

Considered in terms of Korea's entire history, however, the period of 1884-1984 is a very recent chapter. The Korean people have a recorded history of over 2000 years and an oral tradition reaching back into antiquity. Their tribal activities once extended northward into what is now China and Manchuria and southward to the islands which are now Japan.

By the dawn of the first century, the Korean tribes had coalesced into three major kingdoms, Koryu, Paekche and Silla, which later consolidated into one, Silla. This kingdom's boundaries were confined to the Korean peninsula.

Korea has always struggled for survival and for national identity. Often dominated by outsiders, Korea has resisted cultural assimilation. The unique attributes of traditional Korean culture are discernible today in art, music and poetry and in the character of the people.

The first Protestant missionaries to reach Korea found eager listeners. Some Koreans had already heard the Christian doctrine from texts brought from China and from Roman Catholic priests from France. For most of Korea's people, the Protestants' arrival in Seoul in 1884 provided an introduction to Christian teaching.

The methods and the philosophy of Western mission groups will be examined. Sometimes right, sometimes wrong, they have been a part of the Korean story during these 100 years.

The initial enthusiasm with which Koreans received Christianity led to phenomenal growth. The common people, disgraced by foreign dominance and alienated from other Koreans by the corruption and bureaucratic pettiness of their own rulers, turned eagerly to the church. It spread like a match to dry grass.

Once baptized, the Korean Christians began immediately to share the gospel teaching with family members and neighbors. With rare exceptions, drawn from members of the poor classes, new Christians found in their new faith a dignity and hope for justice denied them by the rigid class structure of the late Yi dynasty.

Interestingly, the Protestant ethical message also attracted those intellectuals who opposed their government's conniving with foreign powers. Stripped of opportunities normally open to their class, the intellectuals had "become poor" and shared the common people's feelings of disgrace and alienation. The alliance of common people and uprooted intellectuals, scholars and young students has been a recurring theme in Korea's history.

With external affairs dominated by major powers in east Asia, Korea's domestic life was torn by the contradictions of nationalism and internal corruption. Korea has lurched from one season of tragedy to the next. From the late 1800's to 1945, Korea lived under annexation by Japan. From 1945-1948, Korea was partitioned into two parts and ruled by military governments in the south by the United States and in the north by the Soviet Union. In 1950, a bitter civil war between north and south (1950-53) tore the nation apart. Since then, governments in both places have promised much and delivered little in terms of freedom and democracy.

How has the church in Korea responded to this' troublesome history? What has been the church's role? How do Koreans see these things?

Korean Christians do not have a single view. It would be foolish to make such an assumption. It would be dangerous, and dishonest, to tell only the story of those Christians who resist authority and suffer for it. It would also be dangerous, and dishonest, to talk only about the present success and phenomenal growth of the church. This book aims for reality.

However, these writings are strongly influenced by the view that the church in Korea has been most truly the church when standing with the poor and outcast persons. That is how the church began life there, following the teachings and example of Jesus. That is how the church has reappeared at critical points in the tumult of these past decades.

Growth first came through the common people, the "minjung." The gospel message of liberation and new life fell most gladly on their ears. Their willing feet carried it over the mountains, up the rivers and across the countryside. Their transformed lives were living testimonies to miracles of strength and power.

So it is today, the gospel is translated out of the sweatshops of Seoul and off the factory floor of multinational companies into the everyday talk of young women workers with no background in Christianity. The gospel is interpreted through the experience of farmers in the fields. A truly Korean theology deals with the ugliness and physical degradation which is the lot of most of the common people. This theology emerges, literally, out of the excrement poured over women workers striving for more just working conditions. It's message explodes out of the anger and resentment of the people who feel cheated by centuries of suffering. It's truth echoes and magnifies the thud of a human body against the damp wall of a prison cell.

This theology from the situation, though presently lacking in influence in Korea, could be the starting point for a truly Korean theology. Admitting bias, this book examines "minjung" theology from the assumption that it could become a starting point for changes in Korea.

At the risk of over-simplifying, the Korean experience can be seen as alternating periods, some of reform and achievement and some of weakness, leading to foreign domination and internal factionalism and corruption. Leaders who are unable to lead create feelings of confusion, insecurity and betrayal within the ordinary citizens and alienation within certain segments of the elite.

Unable to rule successfully, the governing group does not direct its frustration toward the dominating outside powers because it is too weak to do so. Instead, the governing group rises up against its own people, further increasing their suffering, called "han" in Korean. Among the people this produces an unfocused anger, a desire for revenge, for "turning the tables," called "han" in Korean.

These upheavals in social values and public life create great anxiety. Understandably, if rational solutions cannot be found, people adopt any number of means of relief and survival. Among these are: 1) outward, silent acceptance; 2) active identification "upward" with those in power; 3) escape into the pleasures of materialism; 4) escape into other-worldly religions or semi-religions which offer security and acceptance. The upheavals also produce situations where the disenchanted "minjung" and alienated intellectuals are forced together, their common suffering providing a new framework for thought and action. They draw deeply on the sources of Korean "soul" for renewed energy to resist internal and external oppression and to build anew. When they succeed, they are brilliantly human.

The material in the various chapters has been written in collaboration with Koreans. It is not a "history of missions" in the traditional sense. Neither is it intended to be a scholarly work. Rather, it is an attempt to offer the opinions of Koreans themselves, except in Chapter Four, which Pharis Harvey wrote, and the work of this writer. The contributors are:

Han, Wan-Sang, former professor, Seoul National University, Chapter II;

Moon, Tong-Hwan, former professor, Hankuk Theological Seminary, Presbyterian, Chapter III;

Pharis Harvey, executive director, North American Coalition for Human Rights in Korea, Chapter IV; and,

Son, Myong-Gul, General Board of Global Ministries, United Methodist Church, Chapter V.

Since the subjects are so closely interrelated, ideas and information from one writer flowed into the assignment of another. It has been a collaboration born out of love for the subject and for the Korean people.

I have rewritten the material to give it a stylistic wholeness, made contributions to some of the chapters, and selected poetry and photographs. I hope that the result increases understanding among Christians in Korea and here in North America. Most of all, I hope that Koreans will recognize themselves in these pages and will feel that our "aim for reality" has been achieved.

THE EMPTY FIELD

What is it here
that is falling down?
What is it that cries out?
Driven before the lonely winds, white waves
drenching the hot earth, the empty fields
of Hant'alli,
What is it that little by little
here is crumbling away?

Like a dream of ghastly, ancient battle places,
above the pile of stones bleached
with the sunlight they shake off, trembling,
the sounds of numerous gunshots pass over   and the
winds descend, whispering.

This is the sound of ancient mountain ranges
falling, of the flowers
and wild berries pouring out
their mad red over the plains

where ruined castles stood.
And this sound of the brass trumpets
tells of the long battle between withering
and the force bursting again into bloom;
it sounds within my ear
and resounds through my heart,
the boiling sound of my blood.

Peacefully,
peaceful as the river at twilight,
the iris burns over the empty fields.
Standing there, the sound
returns
of something steadily
breaaking, something that little by little
is falling down.

by Kim, Chi Ha
from *Poems from the Yellow Earth*, 1970

Chapter I:
THE PEOPLE OF HAN

Koreans talk at great length about "han." Han is especially important to those Koreans who have been kept uneducated, poor and powerless. They refer to life in this world as "han-ridden" or "han-ful."

Han is an unresolved resentment against injustices one has suffered including a sense of helplessness against overwhelming odds. It is a feeling of being totally abandoned and of acute pain born of deep sorrow. Han also contains an urge to take revenge and right the wrongs.

Koreans believe the spirit of a person who dies with unresolved han becomes a fiercely "evil" spirit which can wreak havoc in the affairs of the living. To avoid such problems, one has to pacify the han-ridden spirit and undo the wrongs done while he or she was living. The Jewish people who experienced the holocaust, the Black people who were uprooted from their homes and enslaved in alien lands, the native people in the Western hemisphere who were massacred and dispossessed, and all those who still suffer from such oppression, could also be called han-ridden people.[1]

The Korean people trace their history to the age of Tangun, about 2333 B.C. Tangun, the first king of Korea, is supposed to have been parented by both Heaven, the father, and Earth, the mother. Tangun's mission was to establish and rule the nation. Though much of the early history is shrouded in myth and legend, Korean city-states were referred to in Chinese writings of the 4th century B.C. So it is reasonable to claim that Korea as a nation has at least 2400 years of history.

This chapter presents a description of life in the traditional society of Korea during the 500 years prior to 1910 when Japan annexed Korea. The scene is viewed through the eyes of the oppressed, the han-ridden people, rather than through the eyes of the elite whose perspective dominates most accounts of history.

An understanding of this period can answer questions about why Christianity has been accepted by many Koreans, what it has done to and for the people and nation, and what it could do now and in the future.

THE RISE OF THE YI DYNASTY (1392- 1910)

The Yi dynasty was established in 1392 by General Yi, Sung-Kei in a military coup. Buddhism, which had been the state religion of the overthrown Koguryo dynasty, was replaced by Confucianism, the new state ideology.

The Social Structure of Society Korean society has traditionally been divided, in the order of their respectability, into four classes: "literati," the scholars of letters and wisdom; "farmers," providers of food; "artisans," makers of tools; and "merchants," traders of goods.

Koreans respected the scholars above all others, revealing one of the main characteristics of Korean culture. Koreans prize wisdom, learning and education. In contrast, Japanese traditionally honored the "samurai," the military, most highly, and the United States has admired the wealthy. Korean culture valued intelligence and despised manual labor.

A story illustrates the point. A Korean happened on some Westerners playing tennis. They were running and hitting the ball, working up a great sweat.

He asked his companion, "Why don't they make their servants do all the running and sweating?" To the Korean, any kind of physical exertion was unbecoming for people of noble birth and learning.

These four classes composed the main structure of Korean society. The chart shows how they were ranked.

CHART OF THE SOCIAL STRUCTURE

RULERS

The King

Yangban (aristocrats)

1) the literati — those of noble birth who passed highest national examination for government posts (illegitimate children excluded)
2) the military

THE RULED — MIDDLERS

Chung-in

1) professionals — physicians, translators
2) government officials — functionary posts

Sang-in

farmers, merchants, and artisans

THE RULED — LOWEST

Chun-min

1) outcasts — butchers, leather workers, actors and shamans (religious exorcists)
2) slaves — public and private

The yangban people were given a piece of land by the king once they became government bureaucrats or gained military rank. Farmers made a living by working on the yangban's private land or public land that belonged to the state. Farmers were not allowed to leave the land. Annually they were required to pay, in addition to regular taxes, a certain number of specialized local products. They served in the military or in public works whenever called upon. The yangban people were exempted from all such duties or any other manual labor. Slaves were bought and sold. Their lives were controlled by their masters.

All these social classes were determined by heredity, except for some specific government posts. There was no way to change one's position, no "social ladder" to be climbed.

FAMILY AND WOMEN

The basic unit of the society was the family. The center of the family was the father. As head, he was at the center of the lineage which extended into the past to his male forebears and forward into the future through his sons. The family was extended, not nuclear. It included parents, grandparents, great-grandparents, children, grandchildren, great-grandchildren, all the daughters-in-law and any relatives who needed help. The whole family lived in the same household. No orphanages or homes for the elderly were needed.

Beyond the immediate extended family, society was grouped by clans. The clan gathered together periodically for ancestor worship, called veneration, and for other clan business. On these occasions, Koreans confirmed their blood ties and renewed their sense of belonging. Some properties, mostly land, belonged to each family and some properties belonged to the whole clan. Family records were fastidiously kept. In another sense, the whole nation was considered to be an extended family with the king as the patriarch. Koreans also had the sense of a universal family of all people.

Three Bonds and Five Virtues Koreans believed in three basic human bonds — the bond between king and subject, between father and son, and between husband and wife. All other relations were derived from these. Five fundamental virtues were specified: loyalty to the king, love between father and son, courtesy between husband and wife, respect for elders, and trust between friends.

Moral duties were prescribed for subordinates. The duties were strictly patriarchal and authoritarian. The subjects should be loyal to the king, the son should be obedient to his father, the wife should be faithful to her husband, and young people should respect their elders. The rules and regulations of these duties were so complicated that quite often a person had to consult others for help in order not to violate customs.

A man who had studied and practiced medicine in the United States for nearly 30 years came home to Korea to pay respect to his parents and to renew ties with his relatives and friends. After the first dinner with his parents, he lit and smoked a cigarette. He had forgotten the rule that one was not to smoke in the presence of his elders.

The father was offended but restrained himself from scolding the son. But, he communicated his displeasure through other members of the family.

At the second dinner, the father offered a glass of wine to his son as an expression of affection and in recognition of his son's maturity and achievement. The son refused the wine, not wanting to offend again. But again the father was offended. According to custom, when a son or a younger person is offered a glass of wine by his father or an elder, that person is supposed to accept it with thanks, then turn away from the giver and drink it all at once. The son was reproached again for not observing the customs he had inherited.

Family relationships were the model for all other relationships. The first obligation of each member is to honor and obey the family, the clan and the nation, in that order. Thereby, the whole human community was honored.

The Role of Women   In the Confucian system, the woman's place and work were strictly confined to domestic duties. Women were to serve their fathers until they married, their husbands when they were married, and their sons when they were old. All women were fated to be married, except for those in the class of *"Kungnyo,"* palace women, and *"ki-saeng,"* courtesans. Women were not to be educated, at least not formally. They could never divorce courtesans. Women were not to be educated, at least not formally. They could never divorce their husbands. But, they could be divorced rather easily on any one of the following grounds: if she did not serve her mother-in-law well, had no children (especially a male heir), was lecherous or jealous, had any incurable disease, talked too much or stole.

The highest virtue for a woman was to accept and follow all the conditions of her assigned role.

In spite of such discrimination, a few areas existed where women could and did exert power and demonstrate their administrative skills. For instance, the place and the role of the grandmother in the family or clan was very powerful. She commanded respect and obedience from all her offspring, including the males. She was the boss of the family and the clan in all domestic matters. These women were powerful, skillful managers of their clans.

Sexual relationships between male and female were strictly for the purpose of procreation, preferably male offspring, who would increase the clan. In order to control sexual relationships, males and females were segregated after the age of seven. In ancient Korea, the bride and the groom usually saw each other for the first time on the wedding day. In the early days of Christian missions, congregations would put up a curtain between the male and the female sections of the sanctuary, or build separate wings, in order to comply with these traditions. (See photo insert.)

Many of these customs have been "modernized," although their influence in everyday life is still noticeable.

Yangban Culture   Koreans learned and used Chinese characters for writing, just as Europeans learned and used Latin. The yangban were experts in Chinese classical literature, calligraphy and creative writing. Knowledge of Chinese Confucian classics was the main requirement for both access to higher education and examinations for government jobs. The upper classes also specialized in Confucian literature, philosophy and ethics.

Buddhism and Confucianism were imported to Korea from China by elite scholars around the 4th century A.D. for the purpose of "civilizing" and ruling the populace. They were aimed at loosening the hold of the traditional shamanistic practices. When the Yi dynasty (13th century) adopted Confucianism as the national ideology, Buddhism was expelled from the urban areas to the less inhabited mountain regions. Shamanism was also suppressed. At times a few sympathetic kings favored Buddhism. Shamans were entertained by the women of the court, including the queen. But Confucian teaching was observed. The Korean elite admired Chinese culture, although occasionally they had had to resist Chinese political and military domination. (See the chart of dynasties on page 31.)

Under such circumstances, it was a miracle that *"Hangul,"* the phonetic Korean alphabet, was ever invented. Hangul was created by scholars at the encouragement of King Seijong in 1446. An office to promote its use was also set up. A number of books were published in hangul. The use of hangul was miraculous because the elite class still prized Chinese characters as the written language of learned people. They used Chinese characters exclusively, especially in official and public documents. They despised hangul as the medium for the uncultured, especially women.

The Yi dynasty came to full bloom during the 15th century. Society was stable. Great numbers of writings on history, geography, politics, agriculture, astronomy and medicine were published. Many inventions were developed, among them the first movable printing type in the world, a gauge to measure rain, the sun clock, the water clock, the weather vane and weapons. Among the weapons was the iron clad "turtle ship," again a first. These ships would repulse an invading Japanese armada a century later. The creative surge was also apparent in arts, painting, calligraphy, pottery and music.

DECLINE OF THE YI DYNASTY

As soon as the Yi dynasty was established and had reached its productive stage, signs of decline began to be seen. The decline was caused by the power struggle among the elite ruling class, invasions by foreign powers, the urbanization process and the discontent of the ordinary people.

Political Factions The lands assigned to the ruling elite were limited. The elite endeavored to increase their share by legal as well as illegal and immoral means. The privileges of the ruling groups were so great that every yangban vied for key power positions. Since the elite were scholars, political conflicts automatically involved scholarly feuds among the different schools. The splits between groups became more severe as new generations of scholars increased the number of people involved in the struggle for power and wealth. Inevitably such a struggle adversely affected the morale of the officials, corrupted them and made them exploit the powerless common people all the more.

Foreign Invasions Large scale invasions of Korea by Japan were one of the major causes of the Yi Dynasty's decline and deterioration. Korea's coasts were always being pillaged by Japanese pirates. But, one large scale invasion lasted for seven years, beginning in 1592. The entire country was devastated. The ruling elite were not prepared to defend the nation with the regular troops under their command. They were the first to escape to safety. The Japanese forces were defeated in part by the genius of Admiral Yi, Sunshin with his "turtle ships" and in part by the voluntary "righteous armies" composed of common people and slaves, men and women. They fought a guerrilla war behind enemy lines.

In 1636 China invaded Korea. The Chinese forces captured the capital city, destroying the north-western part of Korea along the path of the invasion. Korea surrendered. Royal princes and princesses were taken away as hostages. Exhorbitant ransoms were paid and unfair treaties were imposed. Again the common people volunteered to fight. They kept harassing the enemy forces behind the lines. The elite and the regular army took refuge in remote areas or meekly surrendered.

The result of these invasions was disastrous. The entire country was destroyed. The national treasury was empty. Government posts were up for sale to the highest bidders. Corruption was rampant. Exploitation of poor people by heavy taxation and extortion was merciless. Many of the poor persons became wanderers and beggars. Some became robbers, notably the famous 16th century "Robin Hoods" who robbed wealthy people and helped poor persons under the leadership of Im, Gukchung.

Rebellions increased both in frequency and scale. The common people resented the fact that the rulers came out of hiding as soon as they were safe and immediately began to exploit those who had courageously fought the enemy.

"Feudalism" Challenged During the 17th and 18th centuries, new developments began to challenge the Yi Dynasty's "feudalism."[2] Advancements in agriculture meant that farmers became wealthier and more independent. Commerce developed with the surplus production. Household industries expanded into large scale operations. Metal currencies began to be used. Even foreign trade prospered. These changes produced an increasing number of wage earners. The more wealthy farmers, merchants, entrepreneurs and wage earners became independent and autonomous of the feudalism system. The yangban elites became nervous and they became more oppressive in their desperate effort to hold on to power.

Also, the number of aristocrats had increased and there were not enough government posts to go around. Those who were excluded from power were compelled to do "menial" work such as farming or studies of less importance.

THE PEOPLE OF HAN

Excluded and Dissenting Yangban Scholars A group of scholars excluded from the power center began to emerge into a new group of intellectuals. They saw the contradictions in society and tried to solve them realistically and scientifically. They were called "Silhak" (practical learning) scholars. Some wrote about new ways of solving rural problems. Others proposed development of industry and commerce. Some studied the history and geography of the nation from new perspectives. They took a new look at the value of hangul. Others made scientific studies of fishery, forestry and medicine.

Some of these new scholars even challenged the orthodox interpretation of Confucianism. But their studies and writings were either ignored or suppressed.

Many of the Silhak scholars were interested in the study of "Western learning," especially Roman Catholicism. They wanted to broaden their knowledge and to solve the contradictions they saw in society. Many of them became believers. But the "Western learning" was also suppressed. The converts were persecuted and many were martyred. This persecution of believers has been a consistent pattern, and in the present period, led to the development of a theology of the oppressed called "Minjung"[3] theology.

Minjung People in Struggle While the yangban system was crumbling at the top, those at the bottom began to resist, revolt and rebel. Often the common people collaborated with the excluded yangbans, newly emerging merchants and local government officials. All this turmoil culminated in the Tonghak (Eastern learning) Peasant Rebellion of 1894-95.

THE TONGHAK PEASANT REVOLUTION

The Tonghak revolutionary forces at one time occupied nearly half of Korea and set up these demands and guidelines:

— Put aside the hatred between the people of Tonghak and the government, and let us cooperate in public administration.
— Investigate corruption among government employees and punish those found guilty.
— Punish the wealthy who exploited the poor.
— Reprimand the literati and the aristocrats who were unjust.
— Burn the slave registration records.
— Improve the treatment of the outcast and remove the headpiece (a symbol of degradation) from the heads of the butchers.
— Allow young widows to remarry.
— Do not collect miscellaneous taxes.
— Do not consider family and geographic ties, but only competence and personal character in selecting government officers.
— Prosecute those who are secretly in collusion with the Japanese.
— Write off all debts, public and private.
— Divide the land equally among those who cultivate the land.[4]

Neither the king's troops nor the Chinese forces could suppress the revolution. Finally, a Japanese task force with more modern weapons came "at the invitation of the Korean government" and succeeded in crushing the rebellion. Today, it is questioned just how freely this invitation was made.

The minjung, the underdogs of the society, fought hard for their rights and for liberation. They also produced a great body of art during this time. Novels written in hangul, paintings, songs, dances, dramas and folktales during this era satirized the social problems. Two of the best-known and loved works of this time were *Hong Gildong Chun*, the story of a righteous bandit with a utopian dream, and *Chun Hyang*, the story of a poor girl in love with an aristocratic youth. The mask dance, a now famous element of Korean culture, evolved at this time. It ridicules not only the religious and the secular elite, but also the common people's own fate.

Through these artistic achievthese artistic achievements, the common people weep over their tragic "fate" and laugh at the whole world.[5]

Loss of Independence By the end of the 19th century, Western nations began to knock on the tightly shut Korean doors. The British, the French, the Germans, the Russians and the Americans wanted trade and territory. The Japanese and Chinese were ever present. In the Sino-Japan War of 1895 Japan kicked the Chinese out of Korea. The Russians wanted to expand into the Pacific region, in search of ice-free harbors. The Japanese wanted Korea as a base for northward expansion. With the help of western nations, especially Great Britain, Japan defeated Russia in 1905.

Finally, with a green light from the United States, Japan formally annexed Korea in 1910. The annexation destroyed all the possibilities of change that had begun to emerge out of the minjung's struggle. Korea was not merely occupied. For the first time in history, Korea completely lost its independence.

The Han-ridden People According to Ko, Eun, a Buddhist poet-monk, "We Koreans were born from the womb of suffering and brought up in the womb of suffering." Suh, Nam Dong classifies the han of the Korean people into four categories:[6]

— The nation as a whole is han-ridden. Because of its geographic situation, Korea has been invaded throughout its history by both the Chinese empire to the north and the Japanese empire to the south.
— The majority of Korean people are han-ridden

people. They have suffered oppression and exploitation under the tyranny of various rulers.

— The women of Korea are han-ridden. They suffered unjustly under the strict Confucian patriarchal system.

— The slaves and the outcasts, at one time numbering nearly half of the total population, are also han-ridden. They were treated as things, as non-beings.

How can this han of the people be resolved? The question was on the minds of many when Protestant Christianity came to Korea. Buddhism had been suppressed for so long that it had retreated far from where people lived and worked. The underdogs did not expect much from it. According to the popular mask dances of the time, Buddhism was seen as senile and unproductive. Confucianism was not the answer. Confucianism was, for the most part, responsible for the han-ridden life of the people.

Shamanism played a priestly role for the Korean people throughout history. But, Shamanism was confined to the resolution of han caused by domestic and personal problems, not of han caused by economics and politics.

People with strong Confucian or Buddhist convictions were not favorably disposed to Protestant Christianity. The small enlightened elite, however, saw power in the Christian religion, power to make the nation "civilized." The large numbers of women, slaves and common people saw a message of liberation in Christianity. This combination of enlightened elite and women, slaves and common people, embraced Christianity. The newly organized congregations offered a new form of community for the people expelled from their families because of their new-found faith.

NOTES

1. See Hyun, Younghak, "Minjung: The Suffering Servant and Hope," an unpublished lecture script, 1982, and Suh, Nam Dong, "Towards a Theology of Han," in Kim, Yong Bok, ed., *Minjung Theology*, Singapore, Christian Conference of Asia, 1981.

2. The word "feudalism" is a term for the medieval European society and cannot properly describe the Korean traditional agricultural society. However, since there is no better term developed yet, it has become a convention for many scholars to use for non-western societies.

3. "Minjung" is a Korean name for those politically oppressed, economically exploited, socially marginalized, and culturally despised and ignored.

4. Lee, Gi-Baik, *Hankusa Shinlon* (Korean History: A New Study), Seoul, Ilchokak, 1976, p. 341.

5. Hyun, Younghak, "A Theological Look at the Mask Dance in Korea," in Kim, Yong Bok (1981).

6. Suh, Nam Dong, "Historical References for Theology of Minjung," in Kim, Yong Bok (1981).

QUESTIONS

1. What geographical fact has had a great influence on Korea's history?

2. What ideology had the most influence on Korean society at the end of the 19th century? What were its major values?

3. What new impressions about Korea did you gain from this chapter?

4. What insights do you have into your own attitudes about Korea after reading this chapter?

5. Could you identify groups of "han-ridden" people in today's world? In your own community or country?

Chapter II:
THE INTRODUCTION OF CHRISTIANITY

Roman Catholics of the Society of Jesus (Jesuits) were the first to teach Christianity to Koreans. The first converts were young Korean men in prison in Japan. They had been taken into exile as prisoners of war by the invading forces in 1592. They became Christians in prison. A few were ordained to the priesthood. But these young men were never to see their homeland again. They were martyred in Japan in the wave of persecutions which began in 1614.

Not until more than 100 years later in 1641 did Christianity reach Korea. The Good News came via Matthew Ricci's *True Doctrine of the Lord of Heaven*, a book written by the Jesuit missionary in China. A member of Korea's embassy to China brought the book back to Seoul from Peking in 1631. Later other books were brought into Korea. The books had little effect until the late 1700's when Lee, Sung Heun, a member of a group of Seoul scholars, went to Peking to see the Jesuits.

The group wanted more information. He returned to Korea in 1784. He brought back more books, Christian articles of worship and a new name. Baptized in China as Peter, he was the first Korean Christian in Korea.

From then until 1884, when the first Protestant missionaries arrived in Korea, the Roman Catholic believers suffered extreme persecution. The government in Seoul was shaky and afraid of foreign influence. Edict after edict was sent out forbidding the new teaching. The first missionary, a Chinese priest named James Chu, was captured and put to death in 1801. The second, a Frenchman, Father Pierre Mauhant, was martyred in 1839. Over 2000 converts lost their lives in this fierce wave of anti-foreign hysteria.

So severe were the persecutions that the first Protestant missionaries found no trace of the believers. Forced into secrecy, the Catholic Christians nevertheless continued to practice their faith.

THE EARLY PROTESTANTS

As with the beginnings of the Catholic Church, Koreans themselves took Protestant teaching into Korea. Suh, Sang-Yoon was among four Koreans converted in Manchuria in 1876 by missionaries from Scotland, John Ross and John McIntyre. Suh returned home in 1883 and began a Protestant witness before Western missionaries arrived. Suh brought with him a translation of the New Testament. He and his friends began circulating it.

Suh was in Seoul when Dr. Horace N. Allen, a missionary physician, transferred from China to Korea in 1884. All things foreign were still under suspicion, so Suh did not approach Allen. Imagine the surprise of the missionaries when Suh came to them two years later, explaining he had converts waiting for baptism by an ordained minister!

Two ordained clergy had arrived together in 1885, Presbyterian (Northern) Horace Grant Underwood and Methodist (Northern) Henry Appenzeller. Another Methodist, Homer Hulbert, followed shortly. According to the story, the Methodists stood guard while Underwood baptized the new believers according to Presbyterian tradition.

The anti-foreign purges ended about this time. Korea gradually reopened its doors to other nations. Those who felt that the nation's future depended on modernization turned eagerly to the Western missionaries.

EARLY MISSION WORK

In addition to the Roman Catholics, the following denominations arrived in Korea before the turn of the century.

Presbyterian (Northern branch) — 1884
Methodist Episcopal, North — 1885
Canadian Baptists   — 1889
Church of England   — 1890
Presbyterian (Southern branch) — 1892
Canadian Presbyterian — 1893
Methodist Episcopal, South — 1896

For the most part, the first missionaries were from upper middle class families in the United States. They were well educated in their professions.

The missionaries came to Korea by invitation and were well-supported by their sending societies. The funds needed to purchase land and set up work were forthcoming. Response was so great that missionaries said they couldn't keep up with the opportunities. More missionaries were needed. This was a constant refrain in early missionary correspondence and reports.

The mission societies came into being during a period of Western expansion. Missionaries followed closely on successive waves of expansion across the Pacific. Being of equal social status and attainment in their home nations, the missionaries felt at home with the diplomats and military officers. Allen served the United States legation as physician and later became the U.S. representative in Seoul.

The early missionaries saw no contradiction in this alliance. However, they were clear on issues of separation of church and state. Underwood later refused to set up a state church at the request of a group of princes, generals and members of the King's cabinet. The group was informed that the missionaries could not organize churches in that way, nor baptize persons for state and political purposes.[1]

Back in the United States people were recovering from the bitter results of a civil war. The divided churches which sent the first missionaries to Korea bore testimony to the sore political division.

But, the United States was on the move again. The Koreans had little reason to trust the Chinese, the Russians or the Japanese. The missionaries felt that the United States and Canada would be good friends for Korea.

EARLY ECUMENISM

A high degree of cooperation among the missionaries marked these early efforts. Perhaps they had the desire to put their own regional divisions behind them. This spirit persisted into the next century. In 1904, the missionaries established a Council of Union and laid plans for a United Church of Christ in Korea.

They "cooperated by cooperating." Their enthusiasm led them to an amazing agreement dividing the Korean peninsula into non-competitive areas for witness. Working in great confidence, they set up union hospitals and schools. Among them were: Union Christian College (later Soongsil University) in Pyongyang; Severance Union Medical College and Hospital in Seoul; Chosen Christian College (later Yonsei University) in Seoul; and the Korean Religious Tract Society (later the Christian Literature Society). They cooperated to translate and publish the New Testament and a Union Hymn Book. They also set up the Young Men's Christian Association (YMCA).

Undergirding this remarkable early ecumenism was a set of principles, hammered out jointly. Called the Nevius Method. They were named for John L. Nevius, a missionary to China who visited Korea in 1890. The strategy plan which resulted from his conversation with the missionaries was simple and sound. It worked for Korea for a long time. The principles were:

1. Emphasis on Bible study
2. Emphasis on spreading of the faith by individual Christians, not professional evangelists
3. Emphasis on self-government
4. Emphasis on self-support
5. Emphasis on missionaries working with Koreans

The missionaries reflected most of the social prejudice of their time. For example, they were highly critical of the "Romanists." Korean contacts were treated with respect. Overt racism was not readily found in their written reports, but racism was reflected in their common Western prejudice against "heathen" ways and culture. This criticism was based on an unexamined assumption. Missionaries believed not only that Christianity and white Western culture were one and the same thing, but were also superior.

To be a Christian meant to discontinue all "heathen" practices. Gradually, being Christian came to mean taking on Western practices. Whatever the missionaries labeled "unchristian" became anathema to the growing Korean Church. Centuries of expression through music, art, dance, poetry, architecture and dress were devalued.

Later, the use of the term "heathen" disappeared. It was replaced by "non-Christian" or more accurate terms such as "Buddhist" or "Shamanistic." Missionaries of the 1920s and 1930s, particularly those involved in higher education, struggled with Korean colleagues for restoration of traditional Korean culture and learning. The work of Helen Kiteuk Kim is an illustration. She was the dean of Ewha Woman's College, her alma mater, and was destined to be the first Korean President of the school. Kim argued cogently and persuasively in her doctoral dissertation (Columbia University, 1931) for the utilization of the traditional Korean school methods. With a reorganized curriculum and redirected objectives, she saw that form of school as the best means of revitalizing rural education and improving economic and social welfare.[2]

To their credit, many of the missionaries worked to restore a balance in the appreciation of Korean culture. They sought the middle ground between the idea that Koreans were God's "new chosen people"[3] and the regrettable destruction of the unique Korean cultural identity of previous days.

The Japanese occupation (1910-1945) was difficult for Korean church members and missionaries. The Japanese demanded strict non-interference of foreigners. Missionaries who were heads of colleges or schools were expected to adhere to all rules and regulations. In 1935, George S. McCune, the head of Union Christian College, refused to allow his school to take part in Shinto worship. He was forced to leave the country.

Korean church members expected missionaries to sympathize with them. A national consciousness was growing, but missionaries were divided about what their roles should be. Some were openly sympathetic to the Koreans, who resisted the occupation and were critical of its acceptance by the United States.[4] Others sought to strengthen Korean friends but accepted the reality of Japan's rule. Still others openly supported the Japanese.

Japan's attack on Pearl Harbor in 1941 forced all United States missionaries to leave Korea. They did not return until after Japan's defeat in 1945. The legacy of the occupation remained. The trauma of these years debilitated the Church in Korea. Missionaries suffered from this trauma, too. The present situation is complex. It would be fair to say that the struggles in the Korean church today are not that different from those of the past. What is the Church? What is its relationship to society?

NOTES

1. Lillias Horton Underwood, M.D., *Life in Korea*, pub. by Young Peoples Missionary Movement of the U.S. and Canada, New York, 1904, p. 253.

2. *Rural Education for the Regeneration of Korea*, Helen Kiteuk Kim, unpublished doctoral dissertation, Columbia University, 1931.

3. "In the little known Hermit Nation the Kingdom of God has won one of the greatest contests of the ages, and not since the time of the Apostles has so much been accomplished in so short a time, for the Koreans seem ordained of God to become His chosen people of the 20th century." Korean Mission Field Magazine, article by T. Newland, March 1927 issue, p. 51.

4. See *Democracy and Mission Education in Korea*, by James Ernest Fisher, Bureau of Publication, Columbia University, New York City, 1982.

Traditional masks used in masked dance dramas which tell of plight of the han-ridden people and poke fun at the upper classes.

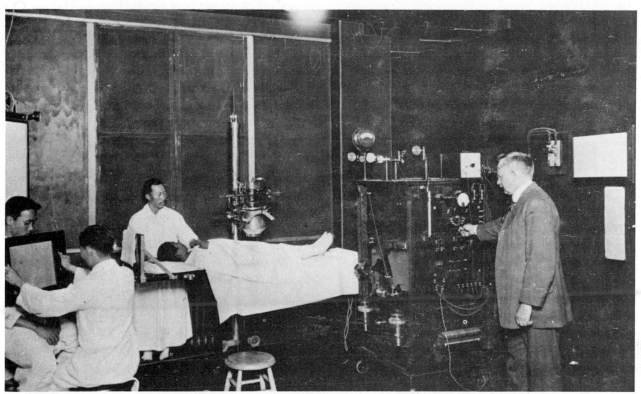

X-ray room, Severance Medical College (early 1900's), Seoul.

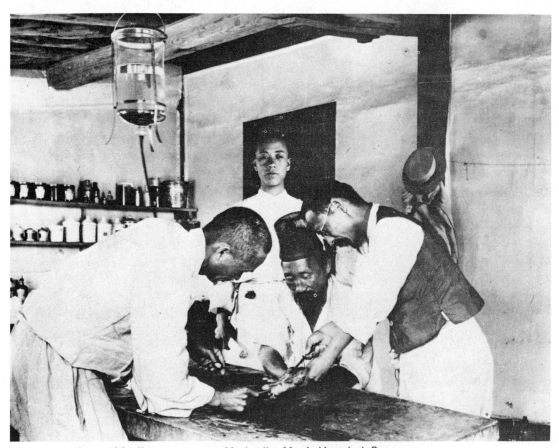

Korean workers with dispensary case, Methodist Men's Hospital, Pyengyang.

Staff working with missionary help to mail out early Christian magazine.

Seoul, April 1919. Laying of cornerstone, Charles M. Stimson Building, Chosen Christian College. Left to right: Prof. Pack, Mrs. H. G. Underwood, Bishop Welch (in rear), Dean Becker and President Anison.

Woman in traditional old Korea dress. Women's faces were not to be seen. Women went into the streets only at certain times.

Man with Ji-kye, Wonju — still a common sight in Korea.

Schoolgirls in big hats, Haiju.

Keija's well, Pyengyang, dug by the King about the time when Samson was performing his exploits in Judea. The King died B.C. 1122.

First graduating class of Ewha, Haktang (now Ewha Womans University), Seoul, 1914.

Four generations of Christians, Seoul, Korea, 1909. Lady in chair is the grandmother, 90 years old.

Three Great Buddhas and their attendants.

A "Devil House" — Haiju.

Y.M.C.A., (under construction), Seoul.

Rev. Kim Chang Sik, the first Methodist preacher ordained in Korea.

This woman evangelist in Korea brought 600 people to Christ.

Rev. Yi Ik Mo and Rev. Pak Won Pak, early evangelists.

Chapter III:
THE SOCIAL CHARACTER OF THE KOREAN CHURCHES

The church is the body of Christ, proclaimed as "good news" to the poor and oppressed. The poor and oppressed are referred to in current Korean theology and social sciences as the minjung. As the centennial year of Korean Protestant churches is commemorated, Christians need to look critically at the history of the Korean Protestant churches from the perspective of the minjung. It is necessary to explore the extent to which the Korean churches in the last 100 years have been faithful to this "good news."

Have the churches been the genuine community of the minjung? If so, how did they come to be so? If not, what are the reasons for the failure to be so? When the Korean churches resisted the dominant groups, what was the basis of their resistance? When they collaborated with the power elite, what was their justification for the collaboration?

With these questions in mind, this chapter examines the history and socio-political character of the churches from the perspective of the minjung. The history of the century will be divided into several periods.

THE CHURCH FOR AND OF THE MINJUNG (1884-1919)

From the very beginning, the Korean churches were minjung-oriented churches. The social class that readily accepted the message of Christianity was the lower class in the last part of the Yi dynasty. Those who were socio-culturally excluded, politically oppressed and economically deprived by the corrupt ruling groups became the first to embrace the good news of Christianity.

The most fertile soil for the seed of Protestantism was found among the small merchants and struggling artisans. These groups were looked down upon by the people of the time. Those who were labeled derogatorily because of the socially defined lowliness of their work received Christianity enthusiastically as a source of a new identity and a new society. More amazing is the historical evidence that those who belonged to the so-called lowest seven classes of occupation swiftly embraced Christianity. (See chart in first chapter.) These were butchers, prostitutes and shamans, among others, who were placed at the bottom most rung of the class structure. They were totally dehumanized.

The readiness with which these "untouchables" became converted caused the ruling aristocrats to disdain the Christian message and see it as a subversive threat. Even the aristocrats who were interested could not bring themselves to "betray their class" by sitting down in the same room to study and worship with poor people.

Mission Policy This appeal to the common people partly resulted from the mission policy of the early missionaries. The "Nevius Method," for instance, was responsible for setting the direction toward a minjung-oriented church. This method was adopted by the Council on Mission for the first time at its January 1893 session:[1] (See also the related discussion of missionary methods in Chapter II.)

1) It is better to aim at the conversion of the working classes than of the higher classes.
2) The conversion of women and the education of Christian girls shall be given serious consideration.

3) Much could be effected in Christian education by maintaining elementary schools in country towns.
4) It is better to translate and publish the Bible and Christian literature in "Hangul," the vernacular language of the minjung, rather than in Chinese characters.

This minjung-oriented mission policy helped to forge the social character of the early Korean churches. The mission was primarily directed toward those who were systematically uprooted, oppressed and excluded. However, what was more significant was the minjung's perception of the Christian mission. The cultural outcasts, the political underdogs and the poor in the late Yi dynasty perceived Christianity as a way out of their systemic subjugation. The early Korean churches rightly and effectively responded to this cry for help and liberation.

In order to understand the eagerness of common people and some intellectuals to join the early churches, it is helpful to recall the socio-political situation of Korea in the last quarter of the nineteenth century. Situated at the crossroads of the big powers, Korea has frequently served as a playing field for the major powers in their attempt to dominate the region. The Koreans have had to endure undeserved suffering imposed by these foreign states and were sometimes involved in unsought wars. Throughout, however, the Koreans have not lost their aspiration for self-determination and national identity as an independent people.

Korea's internal conditions were greatly affected by its powerful neighbors. The power elites in Korea were constantly changing alliances to protect their own vested interests and to reinforce their oppression and exploitation of the people. They intensified the practice of extortion and exacted heavy taxes. As the corruption increased, the minjung's sufferings and pains became that much worse.

Their struggle culminated in the "Tonghak Uprising" which was a historical milestone in the minjung's struggle for justice and liberation. The pro-Chinese ruling group mismanaged the government to such an extent that the practices of selling the government offices became rampant. Unqualified persons who purchased official positions did their best to make profits out of them. Taxes and levies were heavily imposed upon the people. In contrast to the minjung's misery, the ruling groups enjoyed extravagance, licentiousness and debauchery. One poetic description was an accurate portrayal of the minjung's suffering — "Like

the drip of the candle falling on the banquet table fell the han-ridden tears of the minjung, and as music swelled in merry-making so increased the outcry of the discontented minjung."

In 1894, those people who belonged to the Tonghak (Eastern Teaching) staged a revolutionary movement. The Tonghak struggle for justice and liberation was mercilessly put down, however, by the corrupt elite using foreign powers. Many of the Tonghak "rebels" were being chased by the government. They were labeled as "the Eastern bandits." Significant numbers of them turned to the Western teaching — Christianity — for protection.

Churches Accept the Minjung The churches were ready to provide the shelter for them. The number of Christians suddenly increased after the uprising. For instance, there were 777 baptized Presbyterians in 1896, the following year witnessed a tremendous increase to about 3,000 Presbyterians. During the period of 1899 to 1900, 14,000 Presbyterians together with 4,000 Methodists were enrolled in their respective churches. This sudden swell in membership was mainly due to the churches compassion for the socially uprooted minjung. The new message and mission of Christianity was accepted as a sign of hope. A Korean church historian, George Paik, described the situation as follows:

"Political oppression was another cause for the increase of the believers. The people felt that they had reached the bottom of misery: there was no justice in the courts; cruelty, torture, and extortion were prevalent. This political mal-administration and general poverty resulted in dissatisfaction. The splendid teachings of Confucius concerning state and society and fine traditions of the forefathers seemed a failure — By accepting Christianity the oppressed hoped to win lawsuits, and secure justice from the tyrants and protection from the hands of the extortioners."[2]

The social character of the Korean church began to take form against this socio-political background. During the formative stage of the church, the Korean Christians could best be characterized as anti-feudalistic and anti-foreign domination.

It is interesting to contrast this minjung-oriented character of the Korean churches with the more pietistic, evangelical and conservative U.S. missionaries. The churches which sent the missionaries to Korea were not politically minded. In fact, they were very apolitical and ahistorical. But the Koreans were compelled by their reality to transform the Christian mission into one rooted in history. They were determined to change the unjust status quo. From the very beginning Christianity in Korea was accepted by the minjung as a sign of hope and power. It was a religion of "ferment" rather than a religion of "opium."

These underdogs who formed the early churches joined the intellectuals' movement for national self-determination, which in 1896 grew into the "Independence Association." This civic organization aimed at bringing about structural change by instilling into the minds of the people a spirit of national independence. Thus, the public issues this association decided to deal with were politically charged. Virtually all kinds of issues, domestic and international, were discussed in the "Public Meetings" which attracted a wide cross section of the people. From 1896 to 1900, Christian intellectuals developed the movement for national independence and structural transformation of the society.

However, the change-oriented programs of the "Independence Association" were bound to run into resistance from the reactionaries. The association was forced to dissolve. Most of those who were leaders were imprisoned. The missionaries responded to the government's oppression by encouraging the early Korean Christians to withdraw from active involvement in political affairs.

The main motivation behind this "de-politization" was to protect the church in the midst of a political tornado. The Presbyterian Mission Board strongly recommended a policy of separation of religion from politics. In 1901 the Board urged Korean churches to live by the Biblical admonishment to obey one's rulers. Texts which call for submission to the political establishment were recommended to be read and to be used as the guidelines for social action: Romans 13:1- 7; I Timothy 2:1-2; I Peter 2:13-17; Matthew 22:15-21, 24-27; John 18:36.2 This was the first wave of the missionary's attempts to depoliticize the early Korean Christians.

The Church and Politics The policy decision to separate religion from politics was to have a long-lasting effect. Even if the missionaries' motivation for such a decision was understandable, the truth remains that their decision was to have tremendous influence in the forging of the conservative character of the Korean churches, felt even today.

First of all, the logic of the separation policy definitely served the interests of the ruling groups because it discouraged any challenge to the establishment. When the church stressed the importance of the separation between politics and religion, the Christians were led to focus only on personal spiritual salvation. Under this ethos, Christian dualism and partial salvation were stressed. This decision by the Mission Board created a credibility gap between the Korean churches and the missionaries. Besides the resulting tension, the speed of evangelization slowed down. By pulling the biblical text out of the culture which was highly charged with political and social injustice, church growth stagnated. This is a precious lesson to be learned.

THE PERIOD OF JAPANESE MILITARY RULE (1905-1919)

From 1905-1910, Korean society underwent an unprecedented traumatic experience and a most shameful ordeal in the 1905 "Protectorate Treaty" and the 1910 Annexation by Japan. Korea as an independent nation-state disappeared from the historical scene. This period of national mortification brought into view the minjung-oriented and nationalistic character of the early Korean churches. This spirit manifested itself as anti-Japanese sentiment. And again, the church began to grow steadily and noticeably. A daily newspaper, Dai-Han Daily, made the following report on August 21, 1907:

"During the last few years, the Korean people were at a loss what to do because of the government's oppression and Japanese cruelty. Thus the number of people who are being confirmed as Christians increases day by day and month by month. The Korean churches are becoming increasingly stronger, and with this trend Korea shall become a nation of Christians. It is an irony that the government's suppression and Japanese cruel subjugation of Koreans have become the primary contributing factors for church growth in Korea."

This proves again the socially responsive and resilient character of the Korean churches; churches came alive in the middle of structural injustices and persecution.

Along with numerical growth, the structural networks of the Korean churches began to be strengthened. During this period a movement to unite churches began. For the first time there were Korean pastors. Denominational organization was consolidated.

Sorrow at the loss of the country spread throughout the peninsula. People who were totally demoralized sought for a meaningful channel through which they could not only vent their indignation but also express their hope for a nation independent of foreign domination. Korean churches were in the right historical place at the right time.

The "Revival Movement" of 1907 emerged at this very same time. It spread like wild fire throughout the nation. Of course, the revival movement could be interpreted as a second attempt to depoliticize the Korean churches. It can also be seen as a natural reaction to extreme frustration and loss. If peace and happiness are not to be found in this world, then we will look for them in the next world.

However, in spite of all attempts to keep Korean churches from the center of political events, the minjung and intellectuals who had just joined the church never gave up their hope to restore the nation to self-government. Rather, their nationalistic zeal intensified and their anti-Japanese sentiment became more acute.

The fact that the Bible was translated into the vernacular Korean script meant the minjung had direct access to the liberating messages of the Scripture. Therefore, the ultimate source of political consciousness of Korean Christians during this period was the Gospel itself. The Bible was accepted as the book of hope and liberation by the politically frustrated Koreans. Korean Christians' inclination to nationalistic zeal was not a result of a conscious process but of the way they saw the Gospel.

One of the favorite stories was the Exodus story. The reason is quite obvious: the hearers could readily identify with the plight of the Israelites under the oppressive regime of the Pharaoh. The Exodus helped the minjung understand the undeserved character of their suffering. It also instilled in their minds the burning desire to rescue their lost land from the oppressive hands of Japanese imperialists. In 1907, W. L. Swallen, a missionary, witnessed this:

"Egypt is the shadow of the power of sin just as Japan represented a symbol of evil in their situation. Just as the people of Israel got acquainted with the power of evil and sin, the Korean people are learning about the nature of evil; just as the people of Israel became aware of God, Korean people are getting to know God — Thus Christian belief, for Korean Christians, is the power with which the people can be saved. Just as the people of Israel prospered due to God's help, Korean people can prosper even under the Japanese rule, if God helps. This was the subject of ardent prayers of the Korean people."[3]

To the extent that Korean Christians saw a liberating message in the Bible, they became actively involved in various social-action oriented programs of the church. They held prayer meetings for the misery of their homeland and the suffering people. They launched campaigns not to pay taxes and to reduce the national debt to Japan.

The most startling activity of the first Korean Christians was the attempt to remove Japanese domination by "violent" means. Although the churches did not officially join the "people's army" or join the plot to assassinate the Korean leaders who cooperated with the Japanese, Christian individuals and groups took encouragement to be actively engaged in such extreme measures from the biblical message.

One devoted Christian, Oo, Yun Joon, joined the plot to assassinate the First Resident-General Ito Hirobumi. Ito played the major role in enforcing the shameful "Protectorate Treaty." A young Christian named Lee, Jaiyoung attempted to kill the notorious traitor, Lee, Wanyoun. Rev. Chun, Ducky along with a layman, Chung, Soonman, tried to mobilize young people to remove pro-Japanese national traitors by force. The newly founded YMCA (in 1904) played a central role in propagating a nationalistic spirit among the people.

To crack the Koreans' resistance, the Japanese used brute force as well as institutional violence. They installed a variety of repressive statutes regarding the propagation of religion, management of private schools, the right to assemble, organization rules and regulation and the possession of guns and explosives. With these legal tools, Japanese authorities fabricated the so-called "105 persons incident" in 1911 to reduce the Christians' influence upon the nationalism of the people. Influential Christian leaders such as Yoon, Tchiho, Lee, Sunghoon and others were taken into custody by the Japanese police with the charge of plotting to assassinate Ito. This allegation was proven to be totally false. The intent of the lie was to discredit the Christian leaders and thus discourage the nationalistic minjung from staging anti-Japanese revolts.

In spite of these legal restrictions, the struggle for national independence and justice never ceased. The Japanese authority then attempted to manage the crisis by applying the policy of separation between the state and religion. Ito, the first governor-general, was known to have said to a Methodist bishop: "Please leave to me the job of dealing with the political issues here in Korea, but take the responsibility for enlightening Koreans and propagating religious faith to them."

Many U.S. missionaries had a favorable reaction to this policy which they saw as a guarantee of the freedom of religion. However, this freedom could not be enjoyed by Korean Christians as long as their biblically-based criticism against rule by terrorism was deliberately interpreted as anti-state activity by the Japanese authority. Korean Christians saw through the intention of this policy and did not cease to resist Japanese oppression and exploitation. Through such painful struggles for national independence, Korean Christians acquired a prophetic character and a nationalistic orientation.

Nowhere is this more eloquently manifested than in the March First Independence Movement in 1919. This incident is the best historical event through which to view the social character of the early Korean church. Although Christians were an absolute minority in number, only about 1 percent of the population, they played a tremendous role in the planning and nationwide spread of the popular uprising.

THE MARCH FIRST MOVEMENT

By 1910, Japan's colonial government was firmly entrenched. Korean political activities, educational institutions, businesses and freedom of the press were mercilessly suppressed. Japanese language became the official language of the government and courts. Through the use of secret police and military police, the Japanese resident-general was able to exercise total reign over politics and to effectively and ruthlessly crush any signs of unrest.

Korea's economy was reshaped to provide for the needs of the Japanese economy. Industry, transportation and communication were built up to promote Japanese economic expansion and to support the Japanese imperial war machine. The Oriental Development Company was one of the powerful Japanese corporations for the economic exploitation of Korea. Consequently, Japan dominated not only the political but also the economic life of the Korean people.

As the Japanese grip on Koreans was tightened, anti- Japanese sentiment grew. Political oppression and economic deprivation stirred up a strong national spirit. Then came word of President Woodrow Wilson's enunciation of the principle of "self- determination." This word heard around the world ignited the Korean people's will for national independence.

On March 1, 1919, 33 patriotic Korean leaders declared and demanded independence. Over two million Koreans participated in related demonstrations.

Christian Participation Christian churches made contributions to the Independence Movement in two main ways. They provided much of the leadership. Sixteen out of 33 signers of the "Declaration of Independence" were Christians. Some of them were a bit skeptical of taking leadership in a "secular-political" movement. However, it is amazing that a minority religion produced almost 50 percent of the signers. This is especially noteworthy in view of the fact that the Confucius way of life had been the prevalent ethical belief for almost 500 years and the majority of the people practiced either Buddhism or Shamanism. Minority religions such as Christianity and Ch'ondogyo could not logically be expected to play such a leadership role. But they did.

The churches also infused the movement with spirit and vision. The ideals of peace, justice and human dignity were the ideological contribution Korean churches made to the Independence Movement. The churches' contribution made through the provision of leadership and ideology clearly indicates that the message of early Korean Christianity definitely functioned as a catalyst for a movement aiming at radical structural transformation.

In only four days, the demonstration spread to every part of the country. The minjung participated enthusiastically. The Japanese colonial government's statistics on the incident are not reliable. However, even they indicate the national scope of the movement. During the months of March, April and May, 1,542 demonstrations took place throughout the country. Over 2.5 million people took part. The uprising took place in 211 local government districts out of a total of 218.

In 311 areas the leadership clearly took the initiative. Christians led the uprising in 78 areas. Ch'ondogyo believers led in 66 areas. They jointly provided leadership in 42 other localities. This means that the leadership contributed by the Korean churches was about 39 percent. This is also a surprisingly large proportion in light of the fact that Christianity was still in the formative stage. According to the June 30, 1919, statistics, there were 9,456 detainees. Of these 2,033 persons were known to be Christians. About 21 percent of those who were imprisoned were committed Christians.[4] Here again, we can clearly confirm the prominence of Korean Christians' social and political consciousness.

The March First Independence Movement, though brutally put down, brought about significant repercussions. First of all, it encouraged other countries which were in a similar situation of colonial rule to stage peoples' movements for national independence. Secondly, the Korean minjung made it known to the world that they were courageous and capable of self-determination. Japanese authorities and their Korean collaborators attempted to make Koreans feel inferior so as to perpetuate Japanese dominance. They argued that the Korean people were not yet ready for self-determination. The movement proved the utter falseness of such a statement. Thirdly, the movement paved the way for the establishment in exile of the provisional government of the Republic of Korea. This provisional government was founded on the spirit of freedom, equality and justice. It was a modern democratic institution with the minjung as the central agent of history and the nation. This government assumed command of all resistance movements both at home and abroad. It was the first time Koreans established a democratic polity.

In this light, it can be justifiably said that Korean Christians' participation in the March First Independence Movement clearly revealed the social character of Korean churches and Christians as minjung-oriented, nationalistic and pro-democracy. Therefore, it is quite proper to characterize the early Korean churches (from 1881-1919), as socio-politically concerned churches with a prophetic spirit and vision. In brief, the Korean churches in this period functioned as nationalistic and democratic churches in solidarity with the minjung.

DUALISTIC CHARACTER OF THE CHURCH (1920-1945)

After the March First Movement, Korean churches split in their approach to the realities under the Japanese imperialists. The movement was perceived as a "failure" by some in spite of the tremendous repercussion it created when the Korean people's aspiration for independence did not materialize.

Consequently, two conflicting trends emerged within the churches. One was to continue the movement with more realistic strategies. The other was to turn the churches' concern from the secular sphere of "here and now" to the spiritual sphere of the "other-world" and from socially relevant issues to issues of dogma. For some years, the two streams existed side-by-side within the church. But gradually the social character of the churches became weakened. The ahistorical and anti-political character has grown and has prevailed.

The Japanese authority, shocked at the strength of the movement, had modified their policy of ruling by naked terrorism to one of appeasement. The newly appointed Japanese governor-general announced a new policy of "cultural rule."

This policy gained a favorable response from many of the missionaries, who had previously tried in vain to depoliticize Korean churches. This time the churches, weakened by the struggle, yielded to the pressure of depoliticization. A Korean church historian recently protrayed the salient character of the Korean Churches in the 1920s as that of "ghetto." He pointed out three features: 1) Sectarian Protestant movements which lacked historical consciousness; 2) Church education programs which focused on children instead of politically volatile youth; 3) A "ghetto mentality" which viewed Christianity essentially as a Sunday-centered religion.[5]

Fundamentalism and "other-worldliness" took deep root in the soil of the Korean churches during these times of severe national frustration and hopelessness. The Christian God was confined to a sacred Sunday in "time" and to a transcendental other-world in "space." God was forced to rest during the week days from the secular and mundane world and to work busily only on Sunday and in heaven. The spiritual sphere was split from the temporal sphere. And in the minds of the legalistic purists, the impulse to defend dogma grew stronger than commitment to defend the minjung from political oppression and economic exploitation.

At this point it is important to note the political function of this dualistic faith pattern. Western Christian moral codes of that day have encouraged Christians to separate spiritual values from earthly values and to be more concerned about the former. Stress on the transcendental and spiritual tended to make people indifferent to the given distribution of power and wealth. Teaching Christians to yearn only for spiritual rewards resulted directly in diminishing their motivation to press for justice through radical- structural change. As a result, the status quo of injustice and oppression could be maintained.

With such a dualism the Korean churches began to lose their social and historical consciousness. They became reluctant to share the sufferings of the minjung who were the majority. They became aloof from the struggle of the minjung and the intellectuals for national liberation. By emphasizing the significance of being spiritually blessed and equal, Korean churches unintentionally served the vested interests of the Japanese imperialists who had quickly branded the socially concerned believers as "too secular and impure."

Other Worldliness and Fundamentalism

As the realities of sorrow and despair became more acute, the inclination to be apathetic and escapist increased. Lee Yondo's mystic interpretation of Jesus Christ captured the imagination of many. Other worldliness became the first pillar of the Korean Christian's mentality.

The second pillar was fundamentalism. Intolerance and defensiveness are symptomatic of this mentality. Anyone who happens to show any sign of deviation from the sacred credo of fundamentalism is quickly labeled a heretic and relentlessly repelled. Any Christian who seriously endeavors to dialogue with other religions or recognize the authenticity of other religions is readily branded as "impure" and rejected.

Fundamentalists have inherently authoritarian personalities favoring a "black or white" logic. Polarization results when fundamentalistic consciousness prevails. Conflict, dissention and fragmentation are likely to occur. A sense of self-righteousness together with hostility towards dissidents becomes rampant.

The leader of fundamentalism was the Rev. Park, Hyung Ryong, who was a student of Manchen at Princeton Seminary. Manchen was then the champion of fundamentalism theology. Park's students faithfully interpreted and propagated the gospel from Manchen's perspective. Dissention and suspicion arose. They felt that those Christians who were perceived as liberal and who were flexible in their interpretations of the biblical message should be ostracized. They abhorred those who were seriously concerned about the cause of nationalism and humanism. This was why the movement of "new theological thought" led by Professor Kim, Chai-choon was vehemently attacked, first for its liberal tilt and later on for its concern for socio-political issues.

About the middle of the 1930s, fundamentalists under the leadership of Park, their mentor, began to press more strongly on the issue of differing theological views. For example, in 1936, Park's students, who were now local pastors, decided to accuse Kim, Choon Bai because of his "liberal" remarks on the role of women in the church. Kim was known to have said that St. Paul's admonition for women to keep quiet in church was merely reflecting the social custom of a particular province, i.e. Corinth, and that this should not be taken as a universal and absolute truth. Korean fundamentalists brought pressure on him to change his position.

In another case, Rev. Kim, Young Joo was severely attacked for his skepticism of the authorship of the first five books of the Old Testament. He doubted that Moses was the author. As dogmatic legalists gained increasing power within the churches, indifference to the suffering of the people under Japanese rule also increased. Intra-church squabbling intensified as the minjung's suffering and pain grew. It was a tragic paradox.

Meanwhile, the Japanese regime intensified their oppression. In 1931, they went to war against China. Korea was transformed into a "continental logistical base." Japan used Korea's human resources for the purpose of its wars of aggression. In the name of assimilating the Koreans into the Japanese race, this system was changed to conscription in 1942. The Japanese authority carried out the assimilation policy to the extreme point of forcefully prohibiting the Korean people from speaking their own language. They demanded that all Koreans worship at their national Shinto shrines. They even made the people change their Korean names to Japanese names. Thus, the national soul and identity as well as the cultural heritage were ruthlessly and relentlessly destroyed.

Youth Not Silent Under such circumstances, the quietism of the churches is almost understandable. Yet it is not correct to picture all Korean Christians from the 1920s to 1945 as being indifferent toward the plight of the nation and people. In contrast to the church leaders and missionaries who favored the Japanese policy of appeasement and its attendant policy of total separation of church and state, Christian youth courageously raised their voices against their leaders' moderate posture.

Lee, Daewee, a Christian youth, urged fellow Christians to be prime movers of social revolution in an article that appeared in a YMCA periodical in 1923. Later, in 1929, Cho, Byung Ok in an article, "Can a Religionist Be a Revolutionary?" advocated the legitimacy of using violent means to achieve the ideal of justice. He argues as follows:

"Christianity should attempt to transform society by public opinion — when Christians come to judge the camp of injustice to be totally lacking of sympathy and cooperation with the victims, it cannot be condemned as sin to try to solve the problem of injustice by means of force and violence even from the Christian perspective. Hence Christians should entertain a revolutionary zeal in the face of inhumanity and injustice. When there is no alternative towards the realization of justice, but by force, it is not against the Christian truth to bring about structural change by means of force." (Chung Nyun, March 1927, pp. 115- 117.)

Cho, Byung Ok's remark on the relevance and legitimacy of force and violence as seen from the perspective of Christian truth under particular conditions was a clear example of the collective sentiments shared by Christian youth. Looking at their world, they could not help but feel indignant at Japanese oppression. And looking inwardly, the church leaders' bent toward fundamentalism aggravated their disappointment with the church. In the mid-20s, a brand new ideology, communism, landed in Korea. It was accepted as a relevant and attractive alternative to Japanese imperialism by some of the young intellectuals.

Even though the radical tone of resistance against Japanese colonial rule was muted, some Korean churches and lay leaders continued to struggle. The line of the struggle was more that of social movement than of a politically charged nationalistic movement. In one effort, Elder Cho Mansik organized the national movement to encourage the production and consumption of homemade articles. A campaign for rural enlightenment was launched along with a movement to liberate the social castes from unjust social bondage (the so-called "Campaign for Equalization").

Resistance Builds In the 1930s, as Japan forcefully started a policy to destroy the Korean national culture, Christian intellectuals responded courageously. Nam, Kunguk, with a strong intent to implant patriotism into the minds of Koreans, began a campaign of planting the national flower, the rose of Sharon, throughout the country. Prophetic intellectuals such as Lee, Yoon Jai, Choi, Hyun Bai and others organized themselves to protect the national language and Korean cultural heritage from the Japanese policy to erase them.

Some pastors courageously chose to die as martyrs rather than participate in the official Shinto-shrine worship. The Christians and churches involved in these social and religious movements had to go through painful ordeals. Some of them were even left to die in prison. It should be noted, however, that this sacrifice was paid by a minority of the Christian population. The majority of the churches were in the process of consolidating the struggle over dogma and other-worldly concerns, characteristics which emerged as dominant in Korean Christians in the 1960s.

It is not an overstatement to say that the ahistorical and dogmatic character of Korean churches at least indirectly damaged the minjung's struggle for national independence. This observation seems to be relevant still in the current situation.

COMPLIANT PARTICIPATION AND SCHISM IN THE CHURCHES (1945-1960)

On August 15, 1945, Korea was officially liberated from 35 years of Japanese domination. National joy turned to shocked disbelief, for as soon as the peninsula was emancipated from Japanese imperialism, it was divided into two parts. The northern part of the peninsula to be occupied by the Soviet Army and the southern part by the U.S. Army, with the 38th parallel serving as a military demarcation line hastily drawn for military expedience by a secret wartime agreement between Roosevelt, Churchill and Stalin.

This artificial division hardened all of Korean life into two separate and hostile camps. Ever since, it has provided the ruling groups on both sides with the pretext for suppression and exploitation of the minjung in the name of "national security." The emancipation of Korea by the Allied Forces, therefore, did not fulfill the aspirations of the Korean people for an immediate restoration of their national independence.

During the brief period of the U.S. military government (1945-1948), the political arena in southern Korea was gradually dominated by the rightists. At first the centrist parties were growing with the support of the American occupation authorities in 1946. An effort was made to strengthen the centrist parties under the leadership of Kim, Kyushik, but the extremists on both sides threatened to engulf them. Under such circumstances, the U.S. military government switched its support from the centrists to the rightists. This support paved the way for Syngman Rhee's autocratic rule from 1948-1960.

For three years from 1945-1948, the United States wielded tremendous influence in shaping the institutional framework in southern Korea. Even though the U.S. government espoused democracy as an important goal, they did not seek to institutionalize the goal in southern Korea. Instead the United States assisted the authoritarian regime of Rhee through training and strengthening the military. As Professor Gregory Henderson has aptly pointed out, the U.S. government not only failed to build effective civilian institutions but facilitated their undermining by reinforcing the military.[6] In a sense, such a failure paved the way for the military dictatorship of the 1960s and today. To an extent unrivalled by its other post-war occupation policies in Germany and Japan, the U.S. failed to construct viable democratic civilian counters to military control.

In 1948, two separate governments were consolidated on the peninsula. An artificially divided Korea provided the opportunity for political and military action by the superpowers. The two hostile Korean regimes faithfully reproduced the points of conflict and tensions between their patron superpowers.

Caught in the Middle The Korean minjung found themselves caught again in the mesh of world power. Korea became a powder keg. While the stalemate continued and the cold war intensified, Korea had no hope of regaining its unity peacefully. As the hope of reunification became bleak, the cold war mentality prevailed among the ruling groups crushing the minjung's aspiration for democracy. An unsavory political ethos was created. The more swiftly one could foresake one's principles, the more effectively one could get ahead. Moral chaos was the result.

How did the Korean churches react to this reality? One response was compliant participation in and acquiescence to Rhee and the other response was denominational breakup and schism.

The Christian churches' submissiveness to Rhee's regime was based on their perception that he was a devoted Christian. After all, he was a Methodist elder. Many church leaders proudly characterized Rhee's regime as a "Christian Kingdom." It must be stated that the churches played the priestly role in blessing the establishment. Prophetic roles were greatly discouraged. Indeed, prophets in the tradition of Nathan and Micah did not emerge. Of course, the many prophets of the "King's Court" kept saying on behalf of the power holders, "all is well when all is not well" (Jeremiah 8:11).

Even those churches who later took a leadership role in the struggle for democracy and human rights either kept silent or condoned the autocratic rule of the Rhee regime. This acquiescence in Rhee's regime among the churches and Christians can be traced to two main sources. First, those Christians who had collaborated with the Japanese authority enthusiastically joined Rhee's supporters when they recognized that he intended to take the pro-Japanese ex-officials into government services. Remember that by the end of the Japanese colonial period, only a remnant of Christians remained who were prepared to resist. Those who had learned to cooperate with the colonialists' domination swiftly changed their loyalty to Rhee.

Second, those Christians who moved to the south because of the communist persecution and purge of Christians in the north willingly embraced Rhee and his authoritarian policy.

When they came to the south seeking democratic freedom, they found, at least, freedom of religious worship. To them freedom from communism was the most valuable and precious freedom. In the name of anti- communism they joined the political drive to crack down on civil and political liberties and human rights. They were blind to the absence of social and economic justice and political freedom under Rhee. In the eyes of non-Christian democratic forces, the Christian churches were perceived as collaborators with the rightist dictatorship.

The previously forged fundamentalistic character of the churches intensified even more during this period. Such rigidity was bound to cause schism and the breakup of the churches. The Presbyterian Churches were particularly hard hit by schism. The "Koryo" Presbyterians broke up in 1946. The mainline Presbyterians were split into two parts: "Jesus Presbyterian" and "Christ Presbyterian" in 1953. Six years later, the "Jesus" group was torn into two hostile camps: "Tonghop" Presbyterian and "Hoptong" Presbyterian. Both words, "Tonghop" and "Hoptong" mean virtually the same thing, that is, "unity" or "integration." It is ironic to observe that the churches have been broken up in the name of unity and integration!

The more energy the churches consumed in factional strife, the more indifferent they became to the dominant groups' suppression and the attendant suffering of the minjung. This period was indeed a shameful period in church history.

THE PERIOD OF REAWAKENING AND REDISCOVERY OF THE EARLY TRADITION (1961 to the present)

The Korean church did not dare to say anything in the face of the Students' Uprising of April 1960, which toppled the Rhee regime. They had to stand as silent onlookers on this democratic revolution which left hundreds of young Koreans dead. They knew they had contributed nothing to this movement which was the rightful heir to the spirit of the March First Independence Movement.

During this period some church leaders began to feel a sense of responsibility and guilt for their indifference to society's problems. As a concrete sign of their repentance, the Korean National Council of Churches issued a statement urging the military government to return power to civilian hands in 1962. On this occasion KNCC representing its member churches demonstrated its concern for the people's desire for democracy. The message of the biblical texts began once more to be rightfully located in the middle of the Korean struggle.

In 1965 when the Park, Chung Hee regime sought to normalize diplomatic relations with Japan without insisting on an apology for the wrong they had done to the people during 35 years of colonial rule, the people's indignation knew no bounds.

The Korean church responded as one with the people against this betrayal. Christian leaders issued a strong statement opposing ratification of the normalization agreement between the two governments. The statement contained at its end the following resolve:

"We resist all forms of dictatorship, injustice, irregularities and corruption. We reject the impure influence of foreign powers upon all aspects of economy, culture, ethics and politics. We resolve to make a contribution to the historical development of our country with prayer and service led by the Holy Spirit."

The mass media aptly commented that this statement was the first political resolution of the whole Korean church since the March First Independence Movement of 1919. The Holy Spirit moved again in the historical reality of Korea! The Christians were in need of the power of the Holy Spirit through which they could not only rediscover the brilliant tradition of resistance of the early church against injustice, but also be empowered to engage in the struggle themselves.

A sense of urgency ran through the churches. The themes of the youth meetings of that period portray that urgency. The theme of the Methodist Youth Conference, for example, was "Please Send Me." The Association of the Jesus Presbyterian Youth adopted the theme, "Christ Calls for Us," and the theme of the Christ Presbyterian Youth Conference was "Korean Society and Christian Youth." The themes that appeared in the year 1965 indicated a resolute commitment to the mission for justice and freedom.

When Park, Chung Hee attempted to revise the Constitution so that he could succeed himself in the presidency for a third term, another nationwide wave of opposition erupted. On this occasion, Christian leaders again rightfully responded with the people. In 1969, Kim, Chai-choon, the President of Hankuk Theological Seminary (Presbyterian), led the movement to oppose the revision of the Constitution. The government was to belatedly feel the resisting power of the churches by the end of the 1960s. As the Park regime's intent to prolong political power became clear, the regime was confronted by the people's opposition. Ecumenically-oriented churches under the leadership of the KNCC aligned themselves with the struggle.

During this time (1968-1973), the Urban Industrial Mission was born and began to work in unity with poor and oppressed persons. In addition to UIM, KNCC started its mission for human rights. With this new mission thrust the Korean churches were able to show their solidarity with the suffering people. In 1973, the "Theological Declaration of Korean Christians" was issued. This statement is the theological basis for Christian involvement in society. It begins and concludes with the following remarks:

"We make this declaration in the name of the Korean Christian community. But under the present circumstances, in which one-man control, controls all the powers of the three branches of government and uses military arms and the intelligence network to oppress the people, we hesitate to reveal those who signed this document. We must fight and struggle in the underground until our victory is achieved.

"Jesus the Messiah, our Lord, lived and dwelt among the oppressed, poverty-stricken and sick in Judea. He boldly stood in confrontation with Pontius Pilate, a representative of the Roman Empire, and he was crucified in the course of his witness to the truth. He has risen from the dead to release the power of transformation which sets the people free. We resolve that we will follow the footsteps of our Lord, living among our oppressed and poor people, standing against political oppression, and participating in the transformation of history, for this is the only way to the Messianic Kingdom." (See appendix for full text.)

Confrontation In 1973, the church and the state entered a period of confrontation. Whenever Christians have seriously tried to define their position on the violation of human rights and other undemocratic governmental measures, the ruling groups have condemned their criticism as subversive or "pro-communist." The churches' solidarity with the political prisoners and their families and with the growing ranks of dismissed professors, students and journalists has been very much feared by the ruling group. The pastors who were actively involved in UIM and the human rights movement have been harrassed, molested, arrested without warrant and imprisoned. The way in which Christians were suppressed by Park's regime is surprisingly similar to the way in which Christians were mistreated by the imperialist Japanese authority. In actual terms of the weight of penalities inflicted on these conscientious objectors, Park's regime was much harsher than the Japanese government.

It is worthy of note that in the name of God's mission, KNCC has been playing a central role in leading and supporting the human rights movement. The mission of God is believed by the KNCC to be the mission of and for those with whom God identifies. The fact that KNCC has functioned as the prime mover of this mission raises a question about those churches which have not been involved.

Two questions arise: What kind of theological reflection was responsible for some churches' involvement in the movement for justice and human rights? What are the main characteristics and problems of those churches which have stayed away from the movement?

THEOLOGICAL TRENDS

The emergence of two distinct trends of theological reflection occurred in the tumult of the 1960s. One was "secularization" theology and the other was "indigenization" theology.

Secularization Theology The theology of secularity helped Korean churches and Christians to get acquainted with the social reality of an industrialized society. They awakened to find their society at the stage of "saeculum" (history-making place) and "mundus" (the mundane place of the underdog) where Jesus Christ is always incarnated. Without coming to that concrete historical place where downtrodden and uprooted persons are swarming around, it is impossible to understand (or stand under) our Jesus and his mission. This trend worked as

an antidote to the "other-worldliness" of the previous era.

Indigenization Theology Serious theological reflection on the issue of indigenization also helped Christians to understand the merits of dialogue with other religions. Those theologians who were deeply concerned about these dialogues opened the way to understanding the biblical message from the perspective of Confucianism, Buddhism and Shamanism. Comparative studies were encouraged. This indigenous theological reflection worked as an antidote to fundamentalism.

These two theological approaches have helped Christians equip themselves for mission, and particularly, the understanding of human history as the arena of God's action. It is hardly an accident that the current minjung theologians have been concerned about these issues since the 1960s. They studied the theology of revolution, Political Theology, Liberation Theology, Black Theology, the Theology of Hope and evolved minjung theology from their own situation. All of these theologies have grown out of a keen historical consciousness of the concrete context. In passing, it is interesting to note that those Christians who were open to the perspective of secularization have been more likely to join the minjung movement while those who are concerned about the issue of indigenization have seldom been involved, particualrly in the Urban Industrial Mission and human rights missions.

It is regrettable that indigenization theology has not engaged in the concerns of the common people. How can one deal with what it means to be a Korean Christian in a Korean church without dealing with what it means to be a Korean?

There is a second question regarding those churches which stayed away from the present strife with the state. Any suggestion that the majority of the Korean churches have been actively engaged in the struggle for justice and human rights would be misleading. Most of the churches are more concerned about numerical church growth and less concerned about qualitative church renewal. It is a fact that many Korean churches have been experiencing statistical growth unrivaled by churches in other countries.

The largest church in the world is in Korea, the size of the congregation reaching 200,000 persons. It is The Full Gospel Central Church in Seoul led by Rev. Cho, Yong-ki (Paul). The largest Presbyterian Church in the world is also in Korea. A Korean church shall undoubtedly be the largest Methodist church in the world. This phenomenon is uniquely Korean. Church leaders today are tempted to devote total energy to such numerical growth even at the expense of the quality of life in the church as the body of Christ. Great church growth has been greeted with both overwhelming enthusiasm and envy by church leaders in Korea and abroad. Numerical church growth has a problematic character.

THE CHARACTER OF PRESENT CHURCH GROWTH

The expansion of the church is due to several factors. One is the fusion of the now familiar other-worldliness with a new secular interest in "positive thinking."

As Korean society entered a new era of "military rule" with the coup of 1961, the troubles faced by the people and intellectuals grew. All sorts of structural imbalances, as described in Chapter Two, drove Koreans, both Christians and non-Christians, into a state of psychological restlessness. Some tried to overcome it by adopting a "positive posture," while others withdrew into their private lives.

The government, convinced that it could control the people and their activities, began a campaign to sell the political message of positive thinking. Park, Chung Hee learned the value of this strategy when his plan to send ROK troops to Vietnam (at U.S. insistence) succeeded in spite of popular opposition. His "successful" achievements over against the opposition of the people made him a true believer in the gospel of positive mentality. "If we try, we can get it done," was his motto.

Along with the emergence of this political ethos, the non-ecumenical churches began to propagate their own version of the Gospel of Positive Thinking. These churches fell in step with the state in pounding away at "negative thinking." The acts of criticism and resistance were frowned upon and attacked by both the political and religious powers.

Many sales representatives of "positive thinking" were born and they indeed have contributed to a phenomenal numerical church growth. Their stress on "positive thinking" is an important addition to the previous character of fundamentalism, with an interesting new wrinkle. The new groups promise not only victory and equality in the world to come, but mate-

rial success in the "here and now." Being poor is the individual's own "personal fault." No connection is made with the root causes of poverty and alienation. This religiously cloaked message of personal success appeared hand-in-hand with Park's message of the regime's success. Political authoritarianism was mated with religious authoritarianism. This church growth strategy can result in exploitation of the poor and powerless and those out of favor with the regime.

The social character of such churches can best be described as anti-people oriented, anti-nationalistic (or pseudo-nationalistic) and anti-democratic. How can this be said?

At first glance, these groups seem to be deeply concerned about the physical as well as mental suffering of the people. They place great emphasis on "healing." But in being "healed" people are encouraged to be dependent on the "charisma" of their pastor. Decision making is in the hands of the pastor, including the tithes which are expected to pour in.

This is opposite to the way Jesus healed. Jesus' declaration, "Your faith has made you well," persuasively delivers the message that the healed, once powerless, can become "filled with power." Jesus encouraged those whom he healed to grow in their own faith and to become responsible and faithful disciples.

These churches are also anti-minjung in that they form a silent alliance with the rich and powerful. They share the same values of success, "product" orientation and managerial efficiency. They please the ruling groups by deliberately staying away from the affairs of the state. They take pleasure in blessing the powerful at mass rallies. Romans 13:1-7 is often quoted. In turn, they are praised by the government as models of what churches should be.

The new sect groups are also blindly anti-communistic and willing to postpone democracy. They have retained the rigid, cold war mentality of the Syngman Rhee regime. When prophetic intellectuals and minjung were harrassed and persecuted by the government, these churches and their leaders not only supported the repressive measures, but took the lead in branding the persecuted as "pro-communists." They believe that any means can be justified in order to combat communism, so they join the chorus that "collective freedom" is more important than individual freedom; national security more important than participatory democracy and political freedom. The threat from northern Korea has been used as an extremely effective tool to crush individual liberties and parliamentary democracy.

To these "Christian-McCarthyists," the governmental policy of anti-communism is the main business of government. Communism and socialism are always wrong and bad while capitalism is always good and right. They preach that God unequivocally and unconditionally favors capitalism over against any other ideology and system. Such a bias not only distorts the biblical truth; it also helps perpetuate the division of the Korean peninsula.

They also preach a false spirit of nationalism. According to them, the Korean race is so superior and so richly blessed when compared with other races that Korea is the center of God's mission for world evangelization. This reasoning is in line with the claim of leaders of such religious movements as the Unification Church's Reverend Sun Myong Moon. He preaches that Korea is the holy land which produced the authentic Messiah and he is it!

An authentic nationalism supports the people's aspiration for reunification of the divided Korea. Those Christians who willingly or unwillingly contribute to the perpetuation of the division cannot claim to be nationalistic or patriotic Koreans.

One of the lessons which can be learned from the centennial history of the Korean Protestant churches is that only when the church dedicates itself fully to the cause which the people respect and admire such as justice, national independence and human dignity, can the church become the church of the suffering people and eventually the body of Christ. In an unjustly polarized situation, the body of Christ will be whipped and crucified. But it will be resurrected by the power of God. The church as the body of Christ will suffer, but it is a community with the hope of resurrection. Suffering churches are, therefore, a sign of authentic hope for the resurrection.

SOCIAL BIOGRAPHY OF THE "MINJUNG" AS A TEACHING TOOL

"I was born into a butcher's family in the late Yi dynasty (1860s). Our family was discriminated against because in our work we touched animal bodies and blood. We were 'unclean' and treated as outcasts. Legally, we did not even exist. We were not entitled to have our own names, and were disparingly referred to as 'one of the Parks.'

"Of course, in our family we were given names, but always those which told our caste. The same was true with me when I got married and had a son. He was called 'Bonguri,' typical butcher-class name.

"But I had dreams for him. Even a butcher can dream. I had heard of a new teaching called 'the Western way' which actually had classes at night for untouchables and other poor people. We sent Bonguri to that class. He came home full of stories of the teacher, who was also a Western-style shaman.

"That summer, I got typhoid fever. I wondered what evil I had done to be so cursed! I tried everything. The herb medicine of the oriental pharmacist didn't help. Then we called in the shaman. But nothing helped me.

"As a last resort, I gave in to Bonguri's suggestion that I go to his Western shaman. The medicine they gave me worked a miracle and I was cured. In gratitude, I listened to the teaching of the missionary and felt a feeling of awakening. I truly felt that I had been reborn.

"I decided that my reborn self needed a new name, so I threw away the old name and called my new self 'Park, Sungchoon.' 'Sungchoon' means 'Spring has come.' I also gave Bonguri a new name, 'Suyang,' which means 'Bright Beam.' We came alive with our new identity.

"I came alive with my new identity in the liberating power of the gospel. I couldn't wait to get to work for the liberation of my relatives and friends among the 'untouchables.' I was determined with God's help to break out of those age-old shackles, because if Jesus sets us free, we are indeed free!"

Park, Sungchoon became the leader of a campaign to free the butcher caste. From 1895 to 1898, he repeatedly petitioned the government. Finally, they were officially notified that all restrictions were removed and they were free members of society.

Park, Sungchoon was also a founding member of the Sung Dong Presbyterian Church in Seoul, one of the first to be established. Later, he became an elder, the first out of the previous "untouchables" group.

WHAT CAN WE LEARN?

1. **We learn that the early churches were indeed the church of the uprooted and downtrodden.** It is a legacy we should prize. Jesus began his public ministry in the land of the minjung which was described as "the land of the gentile" and as "the people who live in the dark land of death" (Matthew 4:15-16). Jesus came to them as the great light. His

followers were the outcasts, who were described as "sheep without a shepherd" (Mark 6:34).

The early Korean churches were founded on the soil of a Korean Galilee and the liberating gospel of Jesus was implanted in the minds of the Korean "ocholos." This was really a significant encounter between the Korean minjung and Jesus in the "land of night darkness" (as contrasted with the land of morning calm). Therefore, it is not too much to say that early Korean Christians were able to encounter and embrace with their suffering bodies their Jesus in the middle of a concrete socio-historical plight.

2. We learn the connection between personal change (or personal salvation) and structural transformation (or social salvation). The total nature of Christian salvation requires the churches to be the agent of personal change as well as structural transformation. In the age of darkness and in situations of injustice the churches are called upon to bring about justice and light. If it is satisfied with success in personal salvation and decides to stay at this level in an injustice-ridden situation, it works to distort the gospel. The fact the Park, Sungchoon, having acquired a new personal identity by the grace of God, decided to lead a risky movement for liberation of the social outcasts, illustrated this. To him, personal salvation was not separate from social salvation: they were two faces of the same coin.

3. We see an authentic "positive" attitude in Park's life. He was so burdened by the caste system of the Yi dynasty that he negated the legitimacy of the system. Genuine positive thinking negates a negative reality! The biblical prophets exercised this "negative spirit," negating the power of evil kings. This positive mentality cannot be confused with the shallow "positive thinking" which is inclined to bless whatever exists. This thinking which is all the fashion among the Korean churches today tempts the pastors to preach a "sunshine gospel." They fill the minjung with cheap hope. In this context we have to read again what the great prophet Jeremiah deplored. "Even prophets and priests cheat the people. They act as if my people's wounds were only scratches. 'All is well' they say when all is not well." (Jeremiah 8:10-11). Jeremiah was indeed the embodiment of a creative "negative" spirit.

4. Finally, we can learn from what has happened to Park Sungchoon's beloved Sung Dong Presbyterian Church, which is now the symbol of anti- ecumenical groups within the churches. They condemn the churches' involvement in the movement for justice and liberation. Study of the life of the elder Park eloquently points out their misdirection. In this light, the Korean churches with their other-worldly fundamentalism and their tainted "sunshine gospel" can hardly claim to be the rightful successor of the precious legacy of the early churches.

Korea remains divided into two hostile states and the dominant groups take advantage of the threat from the other side to protect their own vested interests. The minjung who cry out for justice, democracy and reunification are certain to suffer. The church as an embodiment of Christ's body must take sides with the suffering minjung and keep its solidarity with them.

NOTES

1. Kim, Yong Bock, "Korean Christianity as a Messianic Movement of the People," ed. by Kim, Yong Bock, *Minjung Theology: People as the Subjects of History*. pp. 79-80. Singapore: The Commission on Theological Concerns, The Christian Conference of Asia, 1981.

2. L. George Paik, *History of Protestant Mission in Korea 1832-1910*, Pyongyang, Korea: Union Christian College Press, 1927, p. 261.

3. W. L. Swallen, "Sunday School Lessons on the Book of Exodus," (Seoul Religious Tract Society, 1907), p.

4. Lee, Manyul, *Korean Christianity and Historical Consciousness* Seoul, Korea: Chisiksanup Co., 1981.

5. Choo, Chai-Yong, "A Brief Sketch of a Korean Christian History from the Minjung Perspective," ed., by Kim, Yong Bok, *Minjung Theology: People as the Subjects of History*, pp. 69-76. Singapore: The Commission on Theological Concern, The Christian Conference of Asia, 1981.

6. Henderson, Gregory, "The Institutional Distortion in American-Korean Relations," *Koreascope*, Vol. III, No. 5, June 1982

QUESTIONS

1. Were you surprised by what you learned about the introduction of Christianity into Korea? What surprised you most?

2. Identify several of the characteristics of the early Protestant Christians and the missionaries.

3. What attitudes of the early missionaries were most commendable, in your opinion? What did they do that you would do differently now?

4. How did you feel as you read about the successive periods of struggle and the efforts of the common people to be recognized?

5. Can you see parallels between the development of the Korean churches in the past century and the development of the churches in this country? Can you identify differences?

6. What do you think about the method of using people's life stories (social biography) as a way of thinking about God? Is it a useful? Is it applicable to your situation?

STATISTICS OF PROTESTANT CHURCHES IN KOREA TODAY

Church Families	Number of Denominations	Number of Churches	Number of Pastors	Number of Members
Presbyterian	29	12,270	17,613	3,999,137
Methodist	4	2,793	3,461	819,725
Holiness	3	1,303	1,713	452,618
Baptist	4	965	1,189	306,984
Pentecostal	7	961	1,585	440,557
Seventh Day Adventist	2	654	255	68,222
Salvation Army	1	173	393	88,222
Church of Christ	3	209	269	37,388
Nazarene	1	148	156	75,191
Anglican	1	66	81	45,284
Others	12	1,701	5,025	847,319
Total	67	21,243	31,740	7,180,627

THE STORY OF KIM MARIA

The independence movement against the Japanese climaxed in the well-planned nationwide uprising on March 1, 1919. The movement offered Korean women the opportunity to be equal partners in the struggle for freedom.

An outstanding example was Kim, Maria, a Christian woman and a patriot. She was born on June 18, 1893, to a wealthy family in Sorai village, Hwanhae Do province. Missionaries of the Northern Presbyterian Church, now The Presbyterian Church (U.S.A.), were active in this area. Maria's parents were baptized by Rev. H. G. Underwood. Soon after their conversion, the young couple renamed their third daughter Maria. Maria's intelligence was evident very early in her life. Her mother's last wish as she was dying, conveyed to her two older daughters, was that Maria would be educated and would study abroad.

The two older sisters kept their promise. Maria was sent to study at Presbyterian-related Chungshin Girls' School. She graduated with an excellent record. After teaching at her alma mater for a short time, Maria left for Japan for further study at Kinsei Gakuin in Hiroshima. Later, she moved to Tokyo to study at Joshi Gakuin, also supported by Presbyterians.

In 1918 Maria joined the Tokyo Foreign Students' Independence Group where she met Hwan, Esther (the Christian name of Hwan Aetuk). Esther was studying medicine there. During this period Maria participated with other Korean students in independence. activities. She once sent some money to the independence group in Shanghai as a representative of Korean women students in Japan.

On February 8, 1919, a number of Korean students gathered in Korean YMCA in the Kanda district of Tokyo. They issued the historic "February Eighth Declaration of Independence." Maria was arrested by the Japanese police, interrogated and severely tortured. She was released without any charges and watched from then on. The Joshi Gakuin teachers realized that she would not be safe in Tokyo. They would have to intervene to protect her.

On advice of her teachers and friends, Maria returned to Korea before graduation ceremonies in March. The school gave her special consideration, allowing her to graduate without taking final exams. She received her diploma by mail.

Kim, Maria not only took home her school books, but a copy of the "Declaration of Independence" which her group had issued in Tokyo. She wanted to share it with her friends in Korea. At the port of Pusan she met her aunt, Kim, Soonae. Her aunt had just returned from Shanghai with news of independence efforts there. Soonae's husband had just departed for Paris to attend a peace conference as a delegate from the New Korean Youth Party in Shanghai.

With her own documents from Tokyo and a secret message from Shanghai, Maria traveled for several weeks in the districts of Cholla and Kyongsang. She learnedof the March First Declaration of Independence that had been proclaimed in Seoul. On March 5, she went to Seoul. She was immediately arrested on suspicion of violating the Security Law. Also arrested was her friend from Tokyo, Hwan, Esther. Maria was acquitted and released from prison six months later on August 4. She was suffering from an upper jaw injury inflicted by torture and from illness that plagued her for the rest of her life.

Their release was celebrated at the home of the missionary Chun, Mirae, the principal of Chungshin Girls' School. Maria's alma mater also provided her with a secure teaching position.

At the same time, the Korean Patriotic Women's Association elected Maria as its president. Lee, Hehyang was elected vice-president. Hwan, Esther became general secretary and editor. The association had branches in many districts and 2,000 members. Late in November, however, the new leaders were arrested again. This dealt a fatal blow to the association. A newspaper carried this brief report:

"The Korean Patriotic Women's Association, organized by Christians in Seoul, has communicated with the so-called Provisional Government in Shanghai and with other Korean insurrectionists abroad since its inception in April. With a headquarters in Seoul and branches in all provincial centers, it has engaged in secret activities such as liaison with the underground group called the Youth Diplomatic Corps, dissemination of propaganda on independence, distribution of inflammatory leaflets, and solicitations for members and for movement funds. . . . Heading the list of those arrested was Kim, Maria, president, age 26, teacher at Chungshin Girls School in Seoul, related to the Presbyterian denomination."

This short item in the Tokyo Asahi Shinbun of December 19, 1919, seems to have been the first notice of Kim, Maria by domestic newspapers.

In June, 1920 the Taegu District Court sentenced the defendents to three years' imprisonment. Kim, Maria was carried into the courtroom on a stretcher.

She appealed the sentence, but the appeals were rejected and her three-year term went into effect. After serving some days in prison, she was released on bail due to illness. She went to Severance Hospital in Seoul for surgery.

The headline in the Korea edition of the Osaka Asahi Shinbun's August 9, 1920, issue put her back in the news. It read, "FUGITIVE KIM MARIA MUST BE PURSUED AND ARRESTED, DECLARES PROSECUTOR KAWAMURA."

Kawamura, Seisui was the prosecutor in charge of Maria's case in the Seoul Court of Appeal. An official of his office had gone to Kim, Maria on August 1 to deliver an order for her re-imprisonment. She had gone into hiding. Reports were that a U.S. missionary and Koreans in the movement had made careful arrangements for her escape to Shanghai. The still convalescing Maria, disguised in Chinese dress, had gone by boat from Inchon, Korea, to Weihaiwei (now Weihai), China. There she met Soh, Byungho (her uncle) who had come to accompany her to Shanghai. Her life in exile began.

The Provisional Government of Korea in China granted Maria the status of representative from the Hwanghae Do province. She was allowed to continue her studies at Chingling College, a school founded by U.S. missionaries in Nanking. From there Maria came to study in the United States, earning a master's degree at Park College in Parkville, near Kansas City. She also studied at Chicago Women's College. During all this time, she was supported by another missionary, Son, Chinju, a former principal of Chungshin.

Maria graduated from the Biblical Seminary in New York City, where she studied religious education, in 1932.

In the spring of 1933, she returned and taught at Martha Wilson Seminary in Wonsan. Later she was elected president of the Northern Presbyterian Evangelism Assembly.

Late in 1941, she collapsed in a coma and never regained consciousness. Maria was cared for in the Pyongyang Christian Hospital. After seven months of unconsciousness and paralysis, her stormy life ended on March 13, 1944, at fifty years of age. Her relatives were sad that she died without witnessing the liberation of the country she loved so much.

On March 1, 1962, she was posthumously awarded a citation of merit for her contribution toward the establishment of her country. A statue of her was erected in Taepyung No, Seoul. For some unknown reason it has been removed.

FOLK CUSTOMS

Folk music reveals two strong characteristics of the Korean personality. The music shows a love and talent for music, but more importantly the music's foremost feature is melancholy.

Women are credited with the creation of many of Korea's most enduring and best-loved folk songs, especially the melancholy ones. Some people suggest this was because traditional society placed many restrictions and burdens on women. Hemmed in on every side, Korean women were overworked, looked down upon, often deserted and left to struggle alone. Korean women through the centuries shaped their tears into song.

The other feature of Korean music is humor. Humor is a common survival tool among people in desperate circumstances. Wicked officials are taunted with malicious wit, and trouble is turned into laughter. Folktales, poetry and masked dramas — all products of the genius of common folk — were also used in this way. Today, it continues as seen in this newspaper article:

SNU Stages Drama on Social Issues

Members of an arts group at Seoul National University performed a shamanistic ritual yesterday on their college campus in which they depicted a series of recent social issues in a satirical manner.

An estimated 4000 fellow students gathered at the school's Acropolis Square as the troupe gave an impromptu performance "to appease the disgruntled souls."

From **The Korea Herald**
October 28, 1982

Traditional Korean musical intrument.

CHART OF KOREAN HISTORY WITH DATES

Tangi* Year	Christian Year	Period	Major Event(s)
1	2333 B.C.	Age of Mythology	Tangun founds Chosun
1212	1122		Kija succeeds Tangun
1779	555		Buddha born
1783	551		Confucius born
2277	57	Three Kingdom	Silla Kingdom founded
2297	37		Koguryo Kingdom founded
2316	18		Paekche Kingdom founded
	A.D.		
2330	4		Jesus born
2705	372		Buddhism from China
2993	660		Paekche falls to China
3001	668		Koguryo falls to China
3003	670		Silla Kingdom resists, unifies Korea "Golden Age of Silla"
3251	918	Koryo Kingdom	Many cultural gains
3567	1234		Metal type invented
3721	1388		Gen. Yi Sunggae defeats Japanese
3725	1392	Yi Dynasty	
	1396		Capital moved to Seoul
3779	1446		"Hangul" Alphabet invented
3908	1575		Court factionalism intensifies between "Eastern" and "Western" factions Catholicism to Korea
4134	1801		Persecution of Catholics, reaction against foreign influence
4209	1876		"Protective" Treaty with Japan
4213	1880		"Tonghak" Religion arises
4215	1882		Trade Treaty with U.S.
4217	1884		Trade Treaty with Russia
4218	1885		Protestant missionaries arrive China and Japan agree to withdraw from Korea, Britain sends fleet
4227	1894		"Tonghak" Rebellion Put Down
4238	1905		Japan Treaty Renewed
4248	1910	Modern Period	Japan Annexes Korea
4252	1919		March 1 Independence Movement
4262	1929		Kwangju Students Revolt
4270	1937		Japan Invades China
4273	1940		World War II Begins
4278	1945		Liberation from Japan
4281	1948		Korea Permanently Divided Into 2 States
4283	1950		North Invades South
4286	1953		Korean Truce Signed
4294	1961		April 19 Student Uprising Rhee Resigns
4295	1962		Military Coup by Maj. Gen. Park Chung Hee
4312	1979		Park Assasinated
4313	1980		Gen. Chun Doo Hwan Takes Over Government

*Korean time is recorded by this system.

Chapter IV:
KOREA AND THE POWERS:
THE HARE IN THE TIGER'S DEN

A Folktale There was once an old tiger in the hills in Kangwon province. One day he chanced to meet a hare and said, "I am hungry. I am going to eat you up."

The cunning hare answered, "My dear Uncle! Where are you going? I have some delicious food for you. Won't you come with me?"

So the tiger followed the hare into a valley. Then the hare picked up 11 round pebbles and said with a smile, "You have never tasted anything so delicious as this before in all your life."

"How do you eat them?" the tiger asked with great interest.

"Oh, it's quite simple," answered the hare.

"You just bake them in a fire until they turn red, and then they are most delicious." He lit a fire, and put the pebbles in it. After a while he said to the tiger, who was gazing hungrily at the fire, "Dear Uncle, I will go and get you some bean sauce. It will make them ever so much better. I'll only be a few minutes. Don't eat them till I get back. There are just 10 altogether, for us both, you know."

So the hare ran off and left the tiger alone.

While he was waiting the tiger counted the pebbles, which had already turned deep red. He found that there were 11, not 10, as the hare had said. So he greedily gobbled one of them up to get more than his share. It was so hot that it scorched his tongue, his throat and his stomach.

The pain was unbearable and he rushed madly through the hills in his agony. He had to spend a whole month without eating before he recovered.[1]

THE POLITICAL REALITY

Tigers abound in Korean folklore, symbols of powerful and evil forces. Heroes in these tales survive and triumph by their cunning and wit, not their strength. It has been this way for all time for the Korean people. Tales were first remembered for their wisdom about how the poor and powerless could outwit their mighty oppressors. Those same tales later became graphic parables of national endurance for a people fated by geography to live in the shadow of world powers.

Korea's history has been marked by the resistance and the accommodations its people have made to powerful and not always friendly neighbors. The Chinese, the Mongols, the Manchus, the Japanese, and in modern times, the Russians and the citizens of the United States. In this centuries-long struggle, a distinctive Korean national character, language and culture have been forged.

How have these international pressures and conflicts affected the emergence of modern Korea? Or to be accurate, how have they affected the emergence of a divided people and two modern states? How are these global issues and conflicts likely to shape an agenda for Korea's foreseeable future?

Today, major global issues are described in geographical terms such as "East-West" and "North-South." In order to understand the impact of today's international relations on Korea, both descriptions are necessary. Korea is truly assailed from all points of the compass. Forced into colonial servitude under

Japan during the first part of this century, since 1945 the Korean people have been divided by outside powers into hostile and heavily armed states. The world's tightest border seals off all contact between the two peoples, even contact within families.

About 40 percent of the families in southern Korea have relatives in the north, but mail does not pass across the border. No messages can be relayed. Most of these families do not know if brothers, sisters, uncles, aunts and cousins are even alive. A steady barrage of hate propaganda from each side describes the other in terms of barbaric behavior. Feelings of immense conflict grow in the hearts of those millions for whom these "hated people" are also family members! The division of Korea cuts across more than the land. It splits the heart of its people as well.

MODERN KOREA'S BIRTH PANGS

The Western powers knocked on the doors of East Asia in the mid-19th century. At that time, Korea was a deliberately secluded monarchy with little outside contact. Since 1392 Korea had been ruled by one dynasty, the Yi clan. A Confucian literary elite, the yangban, governed the nation. In the middle of the 19th century Korea possessed only token military strength.

Korea's neighbor, Japan, had also spent 250 years in self-imposed isolation. The isolation followed a turbulent period in the late 16th century when several hundred years of civil war ended with the unification of the nation by the Tokugawa clan in 1600.

European efforts to open East Asia prior to the 1850s only caused Korea and Japan to seal themselves more tightly against alien influence. By 1850, however, the pressures from the West proved overwhelming. China had suffered repeated humiliation at the hands of European powers. The Opium Wars of the 1840s revealed the extent of China's vulnerability to the worst of Western mercantile interests. It showed Japanese and Korean observers what fate might lie in wait for them if they failed to respond to the Westerners.

Commodore Matthew Perry sailed into Tokyo Bay in 1854 insisting that the Emperor of Japan grant him an audience and negotiate a treaty of commerce with the United States. Perry began a process that permanently altered the political balance of the region.

Japan quickly responded to Western pressure with political reform and acceptance of Western military technology. In 1868, Japan began a path of modern industrial development leading to the militarism of the 1930s, World War II and the current industrial growth.

Korea was ill-prepared domestically for such change. Corruption robbed it of cohesion and common purpose. Agricultural failure and excessive taxation caused repeated revolts by ordinary rural workers.

Forced Treaties   In 1875, the new Japanese Meiji regime carried out a military action against Korea. The Seoul government turned in vain to Peking for assistance. When effective help from China did not come, Japan pressed further. In 1876 Japan forced the Yi dynasty to agree to the Kwangwha Treaty, which exempted Japanese from Korean law and opened three Korean ports to Japanese trade. Japan had done to Korea what it had resisted having done to it by European nations. The treaty marked the end of Korean diplomatic ties to China.

In 1882, the United States followed suit with a "Treaty of Amity, Commerce and Navigation." The Korean court had been told by its advisers in Peking to seek the treaty as a balance to the Japanese treaty. Similar treaties were signed with Britain, Russia, Italy and others.

Korea was thus forced into the modern political arena, but without the benefits of a modern military, a diplomatic corps or any significant knowledge of the outside world. Korea still had little interest in developing commercial relations.

The United States seemed little interested in Korea either politically or economically. The treaty was signed by the United States in 1882, but few commercial interests took advantage of the new relationship.

If the United States was reluctant to press strong relations with Korea, other nations were not.

During the next decade, Japan, Britain and Russia sparred for control of the ports of North China, Korea and Manchuria. In 1903, Japan proposed to Russia that Korea be divided at the 39th parallel. The northern half would be under Russian rule and the southern half under the Japanese. The Russians hesitated. Japan broke relations and attacked. The war was brief and conclusive. Japan destroyed the Russian fleet and pushed the Czar's troops back. The Russian court at St. Petersburg yielded.

Korea Given to Japan   The peace negotiations in 1905 were conducted at Portsmouth, New

Hampshire. The United States once again entered the picture. President Theodore Roosevelt, sympathetic to the Japanese, arranged for a secret agreement to be signed at Portsmouth. The two nations agreed on a division of spheres of influence in East Asia. Japan promised non-intervention in United States control of the Philippines. In return, the United States would not challenge Japanese control of Korea. The Koreans were not even witnesses to this agreement which sealed their fate for the next 40 years.

Resistance to Japan's conquest was immediate, but did not bring about any significant change. Thousands of Koreans fled the country. Primarily they went to China, Russia and Manchuria where they set up organizations to fight for independence.

In Shanghai, conservative and reformist Korean nationalists established the Provisional Government of Korea in 1919. Elsewhere more radical groups established centers of resistance influenced by other revolutionary movements. Even in exile, global politics kept the Korean independence movement from unity.

REBORN INTO RUPTURE

In mid-1945, the Japanese empire was in shambles. Since 1937 Japan had forced the Korean people into an intensive war effort. The program was designed to compel total loyalty to Japan. The Korean language had been forbidden. All persons were required to take Japanese names. Worship of the emperor and other Shinto rites were required. These measures solidified hatred of the Japanese even by Koreans who had once tolerated the Japanese regime. Thousands were driven into underground resistance activity.

All anti-Japanese activity was labeled "communist" by the colonial government. "Anti- communist associations" were formed in every village, town and factory. By such labels the Japanese evoked a great positive bias toward communism in Korea. The Korean people's only knowledge of communism was that it was anti-Japanese. Their access to communist literature or activity was totally blocked. A broad openness to revolution persisted until it was crushed by U.S. military occupation and the similar actions of the Soviets.

Had matters been handled differently, the local citizens' group emerging across the nation might have become a broadly-based national government. However, foreign powers intervened to prevent this.

The Allied powers had discussed the future of Korea among themselves, beginning with the Cairo

Conference of December 1943. At Cairo, President Franklin D. Roosevelt had advocated independence for Korea "in due course." Again at the Teheran and Yalta Conferences, Roosevelt had expanded his ideas for the future of Korea and other small countries liberated from Japanese control. Korea should, he insisted, be put under a trusteeship for 20 years. This was to give Korea time to master the "arts of self-government" and to run its own affairs.

Asians were viewed with a casual arrogance by the United States and other Western powers only a generation ago. The notion that Korea, which had been self-governing for over 2000 years, was not ready to resume its own affairs was based on several elements. Only one of them was racism.

Confrontation Set As the war came to a close, the United States began to view its alliance with the Soviet Union with alarm. The United States positioned itself to confront expected Soviet expansion. In 1947 this position crystallized into the policy of "Containment." Trusteeship by the United States and other non-communist powers under the newly-created United Nations was intended to build a bulwark of democratic pro-Western nations. The United States fully expected to dominate the United Nations.

To assure the United States would have a major role in any trusteeship over Korea, a period of U.S. military occupation was proposed at the Yalta Conference. By the time of the Potsdam conference in July 1945, the war was moving closer to the Japanese mainland. The United States believed a bloody conflict with Japanese forces in Japan and Korea might be necessary. For this reason the Soviets were invited into the war. The Soviet Union joined the war against Japan on August 8, 1945, two days after the atomic bomb was dropped on Hiroshima and one week before the end of the war. On August 15, as the war ended, Soviet troops moved into northern Korea.

The United States not being able to move its own troops swiftly, hastily suggested the 38th parallel as a dividing line between Soviet and U.S. occupation zones. This, it was hoped, would stop a Soviet advance down the entire peninsula and enable a later political settlement. The Soviets agreed and unilaterally stopped their advance at the 38th parallel. The U.S. troops did not reach Korea until three weeks later.

General John Reed Hodge, Commander of the XXIV Corps of the U.S. 10th Army, was named to head the U.S. Military Government of Korea. Hodge was not prepared to go to Korea as a military governor. Nor did he have advisers with knowledge of Korea or the Korean language to assist him. He was chosen simply because he commanded the troops which could get there fastest.

Hodge, who was a political conservative, concentrated almost all U.S. energies on thwarting political and social reforms. The reforms were desperately needed after 35 years of Japanese colonial rule. Hodge, his officers and State Department advisers, turned to the Japanese administrators and a handful of Korean collaborators as their key advisers. Hodge and his advisors took anti-communism as the only criterion for leadership.

The People's Committee and the fledgling Korean People's Republic were rejected outright. Hodge refused even to meet with Lyuh, Woon-hyung, head of the transition government, for several weeks, until after a new right-wing party had been formed even though Lyuh's government was administering large portions of the country.

Landlords, business leaders tied to Japanese interests and a few intellectuals formed the new right-wing party of about 100 persons in all. They lacked any local organizations or popular base. This group joined a few remnants of the largely defunct Provisional Korean Government exiled in Shanghai since 1919 to become Hodge's choice for leadership. Without a local base, the military government was forced to rely on Japan to enforce its rule.

The Soviets do not seem to have had any clearer idea of how to govern Korea. The Soviets established themselves quickly in power with the aid of several factions of Korean communists. They chose to utilize the People's Committees that the United States had spurned. Apparently there was less violence and less resistance to the Soviet takeover in northern Korea than to U.S. control in southern Korea.

Reform-oriented non-communists also participated in the initial phase of governing the northern half of Korea. They were led by the Christian pastor Cho, Man- shik. Gradually, disputes resulted in the consolidation of the power of one communist leader, Kim, Il Sung. The non-communists were crowded out of the government. Eventually they were either imprisoned or fled southward. Several years later Kim's preeminence was firm. The various roots of the Korean communist movement helped the regime maintain relations with both the Soviet Union and China. Northern Korea is virtually unique in these dual-relations among the satellite communist states.

In southern Korea, encouraged by the U.S. military government, other conservative groups organized political parties. In October 1945, Hodge brought back to Seoul the aging Rhee, Syngman who had remained in exile in the United States since 1919. Immediately on returning to Korea, Rhee organized the "Central Council for the Promotion of Independence." Some Korean leaders refused to accept the idea of a government for only the southern half of the country. Rhee, who favored independence even at the cost of the division of the country, came to be the most-favored politician by the United States.

Trusteeship Suggested The idea of trusteeship under the United Nations was opposed by U.S. citizens on the scene in Korea. All Koreans opposed the idea. They had had quite enough of "trusteeship" under the Japanese. However, on December 17, 1945, the United States, the Soviet Union, Britain and France adopted a U.S. proposal for trusteeship for a period of five years under United Nations auspices.

This proposal aroused almost universal antagonism and sparked widespread strikes, riots and other political protests in Korea. This opposition was at first universal until in January 1946 Korean communists reversed positions under Soviet pressure and began to favor the idea.

Thus, ironically, an idea that had been born in the United States as an effort to contain communism found its only support in the communist movement itself. U.S. occupying forces began to organize a separate independent government in southern Korea in an order to prevent the trusteeship from taking effect. Hodge's open support of anti-trusteeship demonstrations sparked a confrontation with the State Department and his offer to resign in January 1946.

The offer was rejected, and Hodge's hand was strengthened. The U.S.-U.S.S.R. Joint Committee met twice to decide the future of Korean trusteeship, but adjourned without results. The United States took the issue of Korea to the United Nations, seeking support for a nationwide referendum to determine the future. With the Soviet Union absent, the resolution passed without a veto.

Political and Economic Oppression It is difficult to comprehend the depth of Korea's problems at this point. Rebuilding was needed at every point. Korea had had an influx of several million refugees returning from exile or enforced work in Japan. Industry was virtually at a standstill because all managerial and technical staff had been Japanese who were repatriated. Agriculture, burdened in the final years of the war with unbearable demands for food by the Japanese, had evolved into a land use pattern that was one of the most exploitative in the world. Nutrition had decreased by almost one third as a result. Food riots and other political turmoils caused the deaths of thousands in 1946 and 1947. Clearly the situation was ripe for revolution.

But the U.S. occupation and its leaders chose repression, not reform. The constabulary was increased and converted into a national police force. Several right-wing youth organizations were formed, modeled after the Hitler *"Jugend,"* for the purpose of intimidating workers and breaking up unions. Right-wing gangs were given free rein to interfere with any political activity that challenged the direction of the occupation.

On several occasions, U.S. troops were called to quell rebellions. On August 15, 1948, when the Republic of Korea was formed there were more political prisoners than at the time of liberation from Japan. It is sometimes claimed that the same was true in north Korea, but few accurate statistics are available.

By the spring of 1948, most opposition to Rhee's right-wing government had been eliminated or intimidated into silence in the south. The same had happened to non-communists in the north.

Opposition Continues Significant opposition to the formation of two separate states still existed. The United Nations commanded an election of a Constituent Assembly in those parts of Korea where a free election could be held. A few observers were sent to oversee the process.

Trying vainly to forestall the election, southern politicians journeyed to Pyongyang for a conference to organize a coalition government of both north and south. That conference, to which Rhee was not invited, voted to form a unified government, to urge all foreign military forces to withdraw, and to reject dictatorship and "monopoly capitalism." Undeterred, Syngman Rhee pressed forward his plans for an election May 10.

Amid such civil strife — at least 589 persons were killed in incidents protesting the election, including 44 on election day itself — the vote was held only in the south. After a few weeks, the United Nations Temporary Commission declared it "a valid expression of the free will of the electorate in those parts of Korea which were accessible to the Commission." The U.S. military declared it "a great victory for democracy and repudiation of communism."

When the Constituent Assembly was convened, Rhee was named Chairman, and later was elected by that body as the first president of the "Republic of Korea," which was declared on August 15, 1948. Three weeks later, the "Democratic People's Republic of Korea" was formed in Pyongyang with Kim, Il Sung as premier. Both governments claimed sovereignty over the entire territory of Korea. Civil war was the inevitable result.

Civil War Korea had moved in three brief and chaotic years from the joy of independence to a division that had — and continues to have — tragic consequences for every Korean family. The dream of entering the post-war world as one free and unified people had been made captive, once again, to the desire of powerful countries to use Korea and its people for their own purposes.

The Republic of Korea (ROK) and the Democratic People's Republic of Korea (DPRK) were formed in a way which set both halves on courses of development that persist today, more than thirty years later.

1) Both were consolidated to protect rigidly held imported ideologies.
2) Both were born under conditions of almost paranoid fear of subversion or attack.
3) Both were forced by this to subject themselves to the military and political domination of one of the super-powers.

In southern Korea, Rhee's government ran into trouble from all political groups who disagreed with the formation of a separate state. Kim, Koo, and Kim, Kim-Shik were widely respected conservative nationalists. Kim, Koo, the most articulate and publicly respected conservative politician, was assassinated in June 1949. Kim, Kiu-Shik went north in protest. Both had fought the division of Korea from the first mention of the possibility. Lyuh, Woon-Hyung, founder of the Korean People's Republic had been assassinated earlier, in June 1947.

In October 1948, a full-scale revolt erupted in Yosu and Sunch'on in South Cholla Province — suppressed at a cost of more than 1000 lives. By April 1949, a total of 89,710 persons had been arrested on political charges, according to U.N. reports.

Rhee's police and the right-wing youth gangs he employed instituted a virtual reign of terror against all remaining critics of his government. Intolerant of criticism even within his cabinet, Rhee changed ministers with such frequency and arbitrariness that his administration was virtually immobilized.

Nevertheless, opposition to Rhee mounted within the National Assembly, which sought to change the constitution to lessen the power of the President. This attempt failed, but assembly elections in May 1950 resulted in a resounding defeat for Rhee's administration. The new assembly began to work on amending the constitution once again. So preoccupied were they with these political developments that they failed to notice the massive buildup of troops in the north. On June 25, 1950, the Korean war burst into open conflict with the invasion of the south by the north.

Seoul fell in three days, as Rhee and his government fled south without so much as a warning to the people.

For three years the war raged on, leaving more than four million dead and millions more starving and homeless. Both the north and the south were devastated. In Pyongyang, the northern capital, hardly a building was left standing. Most of Seoul was destroyed. The United States, fighting as part of the United Nations forces in the south, suffered 33,629 battle deaths. A total of 25,000 Canadians served and 516 died in the conflict. The fledgling People's Republic of China, drawn into the war to protect its borders, also suffered thousands of casualties. The Soviet Union, which had apparently not been enthusiastic about supporting the invasion by the north, nevertheless was committed to provision of millions of rubles in military aid for the war itself and for the post-war reconstruction.

But it was the people of Korea who suffered most. Millions were made homeless. Refugees were repeatedly tossed from one end of the country to the other, unable to provide food or shelter for themselves. Members of the same family were forced to fight on apposing sides permanently cut off from one another by the 38th parallel.

Reconstruction Most of the physical scars of that war have been erased. Modern cities have been rebuilt on the rubble, new farmland has been terraced and dammed. The unexploded bombs and grenades have almost all been found and craters filled. New forests have been started and the ports cleared of sunken crafts. Korea today, on both sides of the demilitarized zone, has few physical reminders of that horrendous period.

But, the Korean War continues to scar the people of Korea and burden them with its legacy.

There are three major ways in which the division of Korea by the super-powers has fundamentally altered life: in the military domination of society; in a dependent economy; and through continuing political repression.

MILITARIZATION OF SOCIETY

Korea prior to the modern period was one of the least militarized societies in the world. When the Yi dynasty collapsed in 1910, there were less than 6,000 troops in uniform and almost no modern armory. Today, the fifth and sixth largest military forces in the world, with a total of more than 1.2 million soldiers, bristle at one another across the wasteland of a demilitarized zone. Korea has become one of the most heavily weaponed places on earth. From having had no influence in government or society, the military has come to dominate politics, to control major segments of the economy and to influence the thinking of every Korean.

For all its talk about democracy, the United States has put the bulk of its financial and moral support into training and equipping the Korean military. U.S. ties to Korea's military tend to undermine, influence and pervert all other U.S.-Korean relationships. U.S. military leaders have again and again interfered in Korean politics on the side of the Korean military. One of the most recent and flagrant examples was in August 1980, when the commander of the U.S. forces in Korea indicated in public his belief that the U.S. would support the bid for the presidency of General Chun Doo Hwan — before Chun had even declared openly his interest in taking political power. Within one week, Chun had forced the resignation of President Choi Kyu Ha and assumed his place.

Top-Down Government Socially and psychologically, the impact of military dominance over civilian institutions can best be seen in the values that operate in south Korean society today. Apparently the same is true in north Korean society, although military dominance is replaced by a single-party structure.

Government is run from the top down, with little means or toleration for the upward flow of ideas or criticism. Republic of Korea governments, at least from the days of Park, Chung Hee (1961-1979), have included vigorous techniques of control and information-gathering. Unquestioning obedience, orderly retention, and conformity with objectives have been the watchwords. The processes of give and take, legal process, compromise, tolerance of opposition and of public opinion have been either disparaged or considered irrelevant.[2]

The professional military class with almost unparalleled power disdain political opposition, which is equated with "the enemy." Dissent, to such thinking, is the same as subversion. Civilian politics, with its necessary balancing of interests and perspectives, is viewed as a luxury dangerous to national security. Military security forces have been placed in charge of suppressinging civilian protest demonstrations. The result has been extreme cruelty to prisoners or detainees, frequent torture in excess of that practiced against non-political prisoners and a virtual disregard for due process in military courts.

The attempt to use military methods to govern a civilian population has resulted in the creation of the KCIA (Korean Central Intelligence Agency, now renamed the Agency for Security Planning). This group spies on all civilian institutions, whether church or union or university. Military means are used to control the press, education, labor and religious circles.

Rewarding The Military Successive governments have had to reward generation after generation of military leaders to prevent any opposition among the generals. Vast public corporations have been created to be run by former cronies of the President. These corporations deal not only in public power and construction, but in petro-chemicals, arms production, steel, shipbuilding and other heavy industries along with lesser government monopolies in salt, tobacco and ginseng. Banking, housing, even textiles and other consumer goods production are also unduly influenced by the need to reward generals with profitable slots among the captains of industry.

Dwight D. Eisenhower warned of the dangers of a "military-industrial complex." Perhaps it is easier now to see the dangers of that phenomenon in another society. In Korea, the growth of democratic attitudes and institutions has been slowed by the combining of military and industrial goals, personnel and values. It has also undermined the security of southern Korea by alienating citizens from their government.

THE LEGACY OF KWANGJU

Since 1980, military domination, and U.S. support for it, have reached new intensity and created a new level of civilian anxiety, and, for the first time, anti-U.S. protests. This conflict will undoubtedly continue to characterize the 1980s.

While military involvement in politics was a problem in the early period of Park's administration, since that time most military leaders have kept to their primary task of protecting the nation's borders. The chief reason for this shift is that Park prevented them from intervening in politics, but they were rewarded in various economic ways.

A special military group came into being related to domestic intelligence. Their function is to guard against insurgency and to protect the civilian government from attack. Under Park this became personalized into his praetorian guard.

Park Assassination The chief figure in this group was Major General Chun, Doo Hwan, head of the Military Security Command in 1979. He was in an almost uniquely powerful position to manipulate the political situation in the chaotic weeks after Park's sudden assassination by his own KCIA chief on October 26, 1979. Less than seven weeks later, Chun had organized a group of generals, all from similar backgrounds, to take over the army. On December 12, they moved 3000 frontline troops into Seoul, attacked Army headquarters and arrested the martial law commander. They forced Acting President Choi, Gyu Ha to name their key members to the cabinet the next day.

Over the next few months, this military group gathered strength quietly. On the surface political liberalization was being enthusiastically debated by a public with long suppressed desires for democracy. In March 1980, Chun was named head of the nominally-civilian KCIA, an illegal move.

Martial law continued in place, but with lax enforcement. Students began protesting martial law and the naming of a military general to head the KCIA. The students took to the streets in early May. Large-scale demonstrations followed, involving hundreds of thousands of students. On May 17, the Chun group struck. Martial law was further extended and the cabinet and national assembly were disbanded. Hundreds of politicians, including Kim, Dae Jung and several other presidential hopefuls, were arrested. A full-scale purge of public life was begun. By the end of summer nearly 100,000 persons were directly affected.

The Massacre When students in the southern city of Kwangju protested the extension of martial law, Chun ordered special warfare commando troops into the city to rout them with bayonets. Several hundred died in the first two days. A full-scale insurrection then broke out in protest against this unprecedented violence. The entire city rose up — men, women and children — using anything they could find for weapons. As a result, surprisingly enough, the troops were forced to retreat to the edge of the city. A week later, however, with the help of troops released from the U.S. - R.O.K. Joint Command, the city was retaken, leaving as many as 2,000 persons dead. Such an atrocity by the Korean military against a civilian population was unknown in Korea. The bitterness of these days has not been eased by subsequent events.

By the end of 1980, Chun had forced the resignation of the civilian president and had taken his place as acting president. He put a new handwritten constitution into effect that guaranteed his power. Former presidential candidate Kim, Dae Jung was sentenced to death in a mock trial; hundreds of other political leaders were tried or banned from public service. Kim's sentence was later commuted to life, then suspended in December 1982 in response to a worldwide campaign.

The nation's newspapers and electronic media were taken over by the government and new anti-labor-union laws were decreed. All existing political parties were abolished and in their place, the government created new groups including a "ruling party" and several decorative "opposition parties." The parties were filled with unknown persons mostly without political experience.

U.S. Involvement This massive military assault on democratic politics was rewarded by the United States on January 21, 1981. On his first full day in office, newly-inaugurated U.S. President Ronald Reagan invited Chun, Doo Whan to be the first "head of state" to visit his White House. But Reagan's invitation was only the final blessing to a process that had, from the moment of Park's death, been tacitly approved by the U.S. government.

Immediately after Park's death, Secretary of State Cyrus Vance issued a statement encouraging the democratization of Korea but cautioning against haste. The United States maintained silence when Chun's group took over the military six weeks later even though it was in flagrant violation of the U.S. - R.O.K. Joint Command structure's procedures for moving troops. The United States did not call for the court-martial or even the censure of the small group of generals backing Chun's move.

Chun's illegal appointment as head concurrently of both military and civilian intelligence agencies was not protested. The U.S. military commander in Korea, General John Wickham, said he believed the Korean military had no political designs.

In May, the coup was mildly protested by the State Department, but troops were authorized by Wickham to suppress the Kwangju uprising. Chun's self-appointment to the presidency in late August was preceded by another press interview by Wickham pledging American support if Chun should take over. Thus, the Reagan invitation in 1981 was only the final act in a 15- month-long transition process during which the U.S. government guided, supported or tacitly cooperated at each critical juncture.

Korean folklore is full of tales not only of tigers and their outwitting by cunning smaller creatures, but of sadder stories involving victims of tigers. These victims are transformed themselves into tigers and then victimize others. Such tales speak with tragic clarity of the situation of Korea today.

ECONOMIC DEPENDENCY: THE COST OF RAPID GROWTH

The division of Korea in 1945 also weakened both halves of the population economically, resulting in each half becoming dependent on a major power in the global ideological conflict. Under Japanese occupation, northern Korea had most of the industry, coal mines and hydroelectric power potential. Southern Korea was the breadbasket, not only for Korea but for much of the Japanese empire. A viable self- reliant economy required both halves to supplement each other.

The 1950-1953 war further disrupted both sides' economies, flattening the northern industrial estates and devastating much of the agricultural land throughout the country, with forests, fields, irrigation structures and dams bombed or burned out.

From 1953 until the collapse of the Syngman Rhee government in April 1960, southern Korea managed to feed its people only because of the huge influx of foreign aid and relief supplies from the United States. In northern Korea, the Soviet Union poured in similar aid. Problems of corruption among the military and business leadership under Rhee undermined whatever developmental impact this aid might have had. By the time Rhee stepped down in response to the student revolution in 1960, the country had barely advanced from the war-ravaged state it had been in at armistice time in 1953. The Republic of Korea's 1960 Gross National Prodcut (GNP), one of the lowest in the world, was only about $60 per person.

The democratic, but ill-fated, government of Chang, Myong (1960-1961) confronted an impossible set of conflicting demands and made no economic progress. The most notable effect of that one year was that it allowed the government's corruption and inefficiency to become public knowledge. There simply was not time, before the military intervened "to set things straight," to get the economy moving.

On May 16, 1961, Park, Chung Hee and his cohorts staged a coup which had been planned since the resignation of Syngman Rhee. Their actions were greeted with considerable relief by a public in desperate economic straits. In his bid to secure public acceptance for this military takeover, Park, Chung Hee concentrated his efforts on "economic development."

Much apparent progress was made during the next decade, thanks to major injections of foreign funds from three sources: U.S. official assistance, mostly as low-interest loans; $2 billion in "reparations" paid by Japan when the two countries reopened formal relations in 1965; and huge U.S. payments to the ROK government for services in Vietnam from 1965-73. These services included soldiers, construction workers and procurement of military supplies. This capital input was critical for the success of a model of development that required heavy investments.

By 1970, the southern Korean economy had striking growth in the industrial sector, although agriculture had lagged far behind. At first the government had tried to build up industries to make goods to replace imports; by 1965 it was clear that this was both costly and unproductive.

A Shift in Policy Under the guidance of U.S. Agency for International Development (AID) advisors, a shift of policy began in 1966 which transformed the industrial structure but continued rapid growth in the GNP for the next decade. The policy was one of so- called "export-oriented industrialization." In this plan, Korea would develop factories to produce goods almost exclusively for export. Korea's international advantage was seen as its plentiful supply of well- educated, poorly organized and poorly paid workers.

In order to guarantee this supply would not be depleted, farm policies were neglected. This caused a historic shift of population from the countryside to the cities of Korea. It was believed by the planners that Korea could gather capital to enable a gradual change to a more highly-technical and skilled industrial society.

Primary trade between Canada and Korea has been coal, telecommunications equipment and fertilizer, according to a Korean government spokesperson.

International bankers and corporations were ready to cooperate in such a plan, especially because incentives to invest in Korea were made among the most lucrative in the world.

These incentives included:
1) a five-year holiday for corporate taxes,
2) no import and export duties,
3) no labor unions,
4) no pollution controls,
5) no limits on return of profits home.

In addition, the government provided factory space, electric power and harbor facilities at little or no cost to the foreign firms. Many U.S. firms were promised exhorbitant profits, off the top, as enticements to locate factories in Korea. The GNP soared. Exports climbed. Thousands of jobs were created. But the cost to the land and people of Korea was disastrous — politically, socially and environmentally.

Political Costs In 1971, while the nation was placed under emergency martial law, the labor laws for foreign-owned firms were changed to forbid unions. A change in the National Security Law made all labor unrest subject to its stringent conditions and harsh penalties. Earlier in 1971, a presidential election had resulted in a near-defeat for Park, Chung Hee by the opposition candidate Kim, Dae Jung. Gulf Oil later admitted contributing $4 million to Park's campaign. Shortly after the election, an attempt was made on Kim's life and, two years later, he was kidnapped by the KCIA from a Tokyo hotel and brought back to Seoul to face trumped up government charges of "election fraud."

These events foreshadowed the establishment of the "Yushin" (Revitalization) Constitution in late 1972, which set the political framework for suppressing any unrest triggered by the hardships inherent in this economic plan.

Social Problems Socially, Korea's development plan caused great dislocations of people, creating vast urban slums and great pockets of rural poverty. Agricultural productivity grew slowly but unprofitably. The consequent rural hardship brought millions of rural people to the cities. Food prices were kept low by government control and by large-scale imports of food from the United States. U.S. food aid made low wages for factory workers less burdensome, but undermined farm profits by lowering prices.

Throngs of country people crowded into the cities, particularly Seoul, which now is home for one-fourth of the entire south Korean population. Its capacity to receive them buckled. Water became a scarce — and increasingly polluted — resource. Sewers were, and still are, almost non-existent. Urban housing, quickly depleted, was supplemented with thin plywood shacks with tin roofs that offered no more shelter from the sweltering heat of July than they did from the frigid Siberian blasts of winter.

Environmental Costs Environmentally, this pattern of development took a toll on the land, rivers, seashore and air. In Seoul, the wealthy buy bottled water. The Han River, source of the poor people's drinking water, long ago exceeded tolerable limits of lead, zinc and mercury, to say nothing of raw sewage. In downtown Seoul conditions are regularly such that breathing deeply can be injurious to the health.

Farmland in areas around industrial zones has been condemned by the thousands of acres and families moved away. Most of the country's rivers are reported to contain dangerous levels of heavy metals and chemical residues from agricultural pesticides. Much of the natural wild life of these rivers and their coastal estuaries have been destroyed.

Ecological problems related to the country's nuclear power development are only suggested by the fact that *no* nuclear waste disposal system has yet been developed and that no public discussion of nuclear safety is allowed. Two nuclear reactors are in operation. One was sold to Korea by Canada. Negotiations for additional sales are continuing. Seven more are under construction and another 31 are planned by the end of this century. Studies of the safety problems of these reactors suggest that the Korean government has deliberately disregarded precautions and banned access to information.

While the world's bankers have lauded the miraculous growth in southern Korea's GNP, an average of 9.5 percent growth per year from 1961 to 1978, the people of Korea are quite literally choking on it.

Foreign Aid Foreign aid was decisive in this pattern of development. In the late 1950s and early 1960s, U.S. aid provided a combination of cheap surplus food and industrial projects such as power plants consuming imported oil rather than locally available coal. U.S. oil companies were among the first to enter

Korea and they have profited handsomely over the years. Almost no U.S. aid funds went into rural development after 1960.

Today, Korea no longer receives food aid. Instead, it has become the fifth largest commercial customer for U.S. farm products in the world. Self-sufficiency in food, which was close to 100 percent in 1961, is down to about 65 percent now. This food aid has tied the Korean economy to the United States in a basic way.

Since the early 1970s, more than half the funds for economic aid from the United States were loans for purchasing Westinghouse nuclear power generators. Nuclear power generator construction in the United States has almost completely halted due to cost and environmental factors. In southern Korea nuclear construction has continued.

In 1983, a House Foreign Affairs Subcommittee investigating southern Korea's political and economic climate asked whether this "remarkable" development had been achieved at the expense of political and civil rights.

Quite possibly, Korea's GNP growth would have been slower under more democratic circumstances. That would not necessarily have been less helpful developmentally.

By the late 1970s it was becoming clear to many observers that the internal problems in the economy would soon lead to crisis. The World Bank in 1977 had warned that the Korean economy needed 9 percent GNP growth per year to avoid social unrest. It was like a bicycle: stability required speed.

In early 1979, a slowdown began and is continuing. Labor unrest among bankrupt companies triggered a political crisis. The head of the opposition party, Kim Young Sam, was expelled from the National Assembly for supporting a group of striking women factory workers. His political home base, Pusan, exploded in city-wide protests. The unrest quickly spread to Masan, Chinhae, and Changwon, all industrial cities in the southern coast. When the troubles threatened to spread to Seoul, Park's KCIA Chief, Kim Jae Gyu assassinated Park, "to prevent a bloodbath" according to his defense, and the country went under martial law.

A MUSHROOOM IN THE SUN

The Economy Under the Chun Regime In 1980, GNP dropped 6.2 percent, the first reverse in more than 20 years. In 1981, thanks to a good harvest, the economy almost reached the 1979 level. But exports have continued to stagnate. The government has talked about substituting domestic market development as a way to compensate, but no actual growth has taken place except in the government-funded construction projects. In 1988, the Summer Olympics are scheduled to be held in Seoul. This has occasioned a flurry of huge projects for subways, gymnasiums, hotels and similar facilities which are being built with government deficits. Most observers believe they will have little economic value to the nation once the crowds have gone home.

Meanwhile, the problems in the economy mount. To compensate for the loss of exports, the ROK government has attempted to induce even more foreign investment, allowing 100 percent foreign ownership in Korean manufacturing, financial and other sectors. New foreign loans have been pumped into the economy to keep it afloat. The result is a certain statistical success: GNP grew by 6.2 percent in 1981 and 5.4 percent in 1982. But the cost of this pattern of unbalanced growth can be seen in other statistics. Foreign debt has also grown, from 28.7 percent of the GNP in 1976, to 56.8 percent in 1982. The Republic of Korea now has the fourth highest foreign debt in the world, over $40 billion by the end of 1983. The following chart shows the rapid increase in debt.

Table I: South Korea's GNP and Foreign Debt

	GNPO	Foreign Debt	Percent
	(in billion $)	(in billion $)	
1970	$ 8.5	$ 2.5	29.4
1972	9.8	3.6	36.7
1974	16.6	5.8	34.9
1976	25.1	7.2	28.7
1978	45.0	15.7	34.9
1980	56.5	27.3	48.3
1982	66.0	37.5	56.8

Unit: U.S. billion dollars at current rate (Sources: Bank of Korea, Economic Planning Board, IMF.)

But it is in the countryside that the economic problems can be seen most graphically. Farmers' prices and farm debt are two important indicators. In 1983, the government's Ministry of Agriculture and Fisheries issued a report showing an increase in farmers' debt to 13.1 times the debt level in 1975.

In one county of South Chungchong Province, a government study showed in 1982 that farmers' debts owed to the agriculture cooperatives alone were equal to average annual farm family income in that county. The reason for this level of debt is the discrepancy between the cost of production of agricultural products and the prices paid for them by the government, which purchases most of the rice and controls prices on other farm goods.

The Catholic Farmers' Federation studies of farm production costs from 1975 to 1982 reveal a stark picture of heightening despair in the countryside.

Table II: Farmers' Loss from Rice Production, 1975-1982

	Production Cost	Govt. Purchase Price	Loss
	per kama (80 kilo)	per kama	per kama
1975	W20,220	W19,500	W 720
1976	27,154	23,200	3,957
1977	32,484	26,000	6,484
1978	45,178	30,000	15,178
1979	54,900	36,600	18,300
1980	71,057	45,750	25,307
1981	69,311	52,160	17,151
1982	76,997	55,790	21,017

Calculated for Tong-Il rice, ROK Government-developed high-yield variety (Source: "Han-bei Keiko o Tsuyomeru Kankoku no Genjo," in *Sekai*, June, 1983, pp. 173).

The result of these changes is an alarming rate of increase in tenant-farming. Until 1980, Republic of Korea law prohibited the holding of more agricultural land than could be farmed by the owner. This law, part of the land reform of the 1950s, kept the amount of tenant farming in check until recently. With the changes in the law in 1980 under Chun, the problems of tenant farming have dramatically increased as this table shows.

Table III: Percent of Total Agricultural Land Tilled

	by Tenants	by Owners
1960	26.4%	73.6%
1970	33.5	66.5
1980	37.1	62.9
1981	46.4	53.6

(Source: same as for Table II)

The "economic miracle" has begun to show its weakness, like a mushroom under the harsh light of the sun. Extremely sensitive to fluctuations in the international market, the Korean economy trembled with each new trade barrier erected by protectionist countries of the West.

The government, which had built its plans on the basis of absolute political control, found it more and more risky to permit any liberalizations. Critics grew increasingly cynical and skeptical about the role of the United States in supporting such a government and economic situation. Trouble brewed.

THE ATROPHY OF POLITICS

In the early days of the Republic of Korea, political institutions were poorly developed. Thirty-five years of colonialism had been followed by the devastation of war. The country was poor and feared for its security.

Ironically, the more Korea has advanced economically and militarily, the more it has retreated politically. Since 1980, under the Chun, Doo Whan regime, the systematic suppression of freedom and the destruction of a pluralistic society have increased. The institutions that nurture the growth of freedom have been successively co-opted or destroyed. What has happened to the press, local government, rural organizations, labor unions, universities and political parties?

The Media Park attempted to control the press. About 70 reporters were forced out of their jobs in 1974-75. However, this effort was eclipsed by the purge of as many as 700 reporters by Chun in the summer of 1980. At the same time, the government forced the merger of all television networks into one government- controlled system, merged all news services into one government-controlled wire service, forced the Christian Broadcasting Service to end its coverage of news, and established an advertising agency through which all newspaper advertising had to be channeled. In every newsroom, colonels direct the news. Press guidances are issued regularly, setting the boundaries of what can be reported. The result: a totally captive press.

Local Government During 1948-60 local and provincial assemblies were directly elected. Mayors and provincial governors were elected by their assemblies. In 1959, Syngman Rhee changed the law to allow himself to appoint mayors and governors. This was reversed during the brief one year of the Chang Myong government in 1960-61. Park's coup in 1961 stopped all local autonomy. Arguing that national security required strong central authority, Park began to directly appoint all officials below the level of national assembly member. In 1972, he restructured the assembly to allow one-third of its members to be presidentially appointed.

Today, the same excuse of national security is used to block any move toward local political autonomy. The only officials directly elected in Korea today are two-thirds of the members of the National Assembly.

Rural Organizations The rural population has been traditionally ignored by Republic of Korea governments. During the '70s, when unbalanced development programs were causing increased rural misery, it became necessary for the Park government to react. The New Village (Semaul) Movement was established. The villages received a government-controlled agricultural cooperative, loans for farm housing, village improvement projects and a few self help industrial projects for off-season work.

As in the political structure, all decisions were made at the top and imposed on farmers. The local Semaul organizations have not been used as training grounds for more self-generated village political life. Instead they were units to carry out the orders from a central authority and to prevent the development of any independent organizations. Both Catholic and Protestant farmers' organizations have been harassed and intimidated by government officials. Their local members and officers have been arrested, their leaders have been subject to pro-communist rumors, and their national meetings have been prevented.

Labor Unions Industrial workers have been subject to the most thorough oppression. In the 1940s, most known labor leaders were imprisoned under the U.S. military rule. In the 1950s, despite much repression, the labor movement began to grow. Then in 1961, all existing labor organizations were banned and replaced by the government-controlled Federation of Korean Trade Unions.

During the next 19 years, this union dominated labor, and the government dominated it through KCIA infiltration. Despite this, in factory after factory local unions achieved real bargaining strength. In a few factories, workers were able to elect their own officers.

In 1980, this, too, was destroyed. Unions were banned and more than 300 union officers were purged. The laws were changed to prevent national unions from engaging in local organizing. Companies were encouraged to fire union officers. Churches were prevented by law from organizing or aiding workers.

The result: by 1983, union membership in Korea has reportedly plunged from one million to under 100,000. There are no known active union locals. In the few unions that remained strong until 1982, thugs were set loose on union officers; kidnappings, murder threats and destruction of union offices were encouraged. Union officers who protested were themselves imprisoned, "for illegal assembly." The labor movement has been destroyed, or driven underground.

The Universities Students in Korea have acted as the political conscience of the nation. In 1960, the student revolution cost 171 lives, but brought down the corrupt Rhee regime. During the Park period, students demonstrated at critical points — to prevent the "normalization" of relations with Japan in 1965, to protest the 1969 constitutional change that allowed Park a third term, and to protest the Yushin Constitution of 1972. By the '70s, thousands of students had been expelled or imprisoned, hundreds subjected to harsh torture. Campuses were put under tight surveillance by plainclothes policemen. From time to time, bus loads of riot police were stationed outside university gates.

The Chun regime, however, has greatly intensified its control over university students. In 1980, the government decreed that universities must enroll one-third more students than could graduate. An intensely competitive environment on campuses was created. Every university teacher was assigned a group of students for whose political activity he or she must be responsible. If the students engage in demonstrations, their advisors are censured or fired. This has virtually stopped all communication between students and teachers. All independent student circles are prohibited. In every village, local residents are encouraged to report any gathering of students or other young persons. Hundreds of books previously approved by government censors have been removed even from research libraries and from public bookstores. On every campus today, from 100 to 200 plainclothes police — many of whom are former hoodlums — attend classes and break up violently any gathering of more than two students.

In spite of these measures, the number of student protests against the government has multiplied each year. In the spring of 1983, more than 100 demonstrations took place, three times the number of the previous year. More than 300 students were in prison on political charges. The student movement, rather than being suppressed, had become bolder and more radical.

But in 1983, a new form of pressure was added. Several politically active women students were raped or sexually assaulted by government security agents on campus. These outrages generated deep, burning hostility among the students. One student expressed their anger:

"THIS WHOLE GENERATION HAS BEEN RAPED! That is because America is raping this whole Korean peninsula. Not only is the Korean press silent, the entire world's press is silently cooperating in this rape. Nor is that all. Students are every day risking their lives. But look at our cowardly professors. . . . They are committed to nothing, neither resistance nor even suicide. They are without hope. 'The students are turning Red,' they mutter calmly, while they give their consent to these deeply criminal times. Occasionally they beg for our sympathy, 'because,' they say, 'we're helpless.' But it is no wonder we are being raped. To try to succeed in today's world is to ask to be raped."[3]

Political Parties All existing political parties have been banned since 1980. In the opening weeks of 1981, the new government of Chun, created new political parties out of whole cloth. Not just a "ruling" party, but several "opposition" parties were mandated. More than 500 politicians were banned from participation in politics for 8 years. In 1983, the number of banned politicians was reduced to 307. This number still included all politicians or other public figures who had been openly critical of the Park, Chung Hee government. The new hand-picked "opposition" had not yet become a political factor.

The dismantling of political institutions in south Korea has retarded political development, but has not destroyed the popular desire for a more democratic form of government. In 1980, over 80 percent of a national public opinion sample taken by a university indicated the return of democracy was the most urgent national business. In 1983, nearly the same percentage expressed the same priority again. With all legitimate channels of expression blocked, it seemed certain that radical political activism would grow.

CONCLUSION

At this point, our story of the Tiger and the Hare ends. The Republic of Korea has survived its modern century of invasion, control, intervention, alliances, wars and economic domination by the various global powers. But the price has been paid, tragically, by the ordinary people of Korea. Whether the next generation of Korean people will triumph over the tigers among them is a tale not yet told. Its beginnings can be sensed in the struggles for democracy, for human rights and for economic justice, which are the subject of the chapters to follow.

NOTES

1. Zong, In-Sob, *Folk Tales From Korea* (Seoul, Korea: Hollyim Press) p. 157-158.

2. Gregory Henderson, "The Institutional Distortion in American Korean Relations," an unpublished paper, 1982, p. 6.

3. *Sekai*, June, 1983.

QUESTIONS

1. Look at the Korean use of humor in dealing with difficulty in the folk story which begins the chapter. Who does the tiger represent? The hare? What do you suppose the pebbles might represent?

2. Which countries have been most influential in Korea throughout her history?

3. How do you feel about your country's involvement with Korea? What are the positive points? What are the negative points?

4. What insights have you gained into the role Japan has played in Korea?

5. Trace the causes for the increasing militarization of Korean society. How has the United States been involved? What impact might this be having on the Korean churches?

Modern Seoul.

TYPICAL MYTHS, LEGENDS AND FOLK STORIES

The Myth of Tangun In the early days of Korea, before there were any human beings, there were tigers and bears. There was one tiger and one bear who lived together in the same cave.

They prayed to God ("Hananim") to transform them into human beings. So God gave each of them twenty cloves of garlic and some mugwort and told them to eat it and say prayers for a period of 100 days.

The bear followed God's instructions faithfully, and at the end of only the 37th day, was transformed into a beautiful woman. But the tiger failed to do what God had commanded and remained a tiger.

Now the beautiful woman had no man to marry. She prayed under a mahogany tree that she might conceive a child. God heard her prayers, took pity on her and gave her a son. The son was named Tangun and he grew up to be the first king of Korea. He made Pyungyang his capital and called his land Chosun. It is said that he lived for 1,408 years.

Myth of the Creation of the Earth The story is told that once there was a young girl who was greatly loved by the king of one of the countries in the heavens. One day she lost a favorite ring and was very upset. The king would do anything to make her happy, so he had everyone in the kingdom searching for the lost ring.

But it couldn't be found anywhere. Thinking that it must have fallen out of the heavens and down to earth, the king sent a giant down to look for it there.

Now at that time the earth was nothing but mud. As the giant searched for the ring, he raised up huge piles of mud which became mountains, and the excavated areas became the seas. The places where he scratched with his fingers became rivers and where he smoothed the mud out with his palms became the flat plains.

The Legend of the Unjin Buddha There is a statue of Buddha in the village of Unjin in South Chungchong Province. It is famous for its great size. It stands 74 feet high and wears a crown that is seven feet tall. A legend is told of how this statue came to be built. It all happened over 1,000 years ago in the reign of King Kwangjong of the Koryu kingdom.

It seems that a woman from the village went out to the hills nearby to gather firewood. While gathering the wood, she heard a strange sound. Turning around, she saw that a giant rock had sprung up out of the earth.

She ran back to the village with the news. The story reached the court and finally, the king heard it. He interpreted it as a divine message from Buddha. Wanting to make the best possible use of the strange stone, he summoned stonemasons from all over the kingdom to go to Unjin and make a statue of Buddha out of it. He assigned the monk Hemyong to supervise the carving.

As the days passed and the Buddha's image began to take shape, everything was fine except that the monk could not figure out how to get the huge head and crown up on the body. One day, the priest saw a child playing in the street. Suddenly, he saw the solution to the problem right before his very eyes! For the child was playing with wet clay, making a statue of Buddha. He took other clay and make a mound around the body. Then he rolled the head and crown up the side of the mound and put them in place.

The legend has it that the child was really Manjuri, the god of wisdom and intelligence, in disguise. Anyway, you can see the statue of Buddha there in Unjin today.

The Story of the Priest and the Tiger Once upon a time, a certain scholar was traveling along a mountain road. He decided to take a little rest and sat down by some big rocks. Imagine his surprise when he saw the tail of a huge tiger sticking out between the rocks! He let out a yell and jumped up.

His cry woke up the tiger, who looked around for the source of the disturbance. He was just about to jump when the priest grabbed hold of his tail and pulled it between the rocks. A mighty tug-of-war then took place.

Just then a Buddhist priest happened to come by. The scholar was overjoyed. He called to the priest to kill the tiger with his walking staff. But the priest shook his head and said he could not, reminding the scholar that Buddha's teaching forbade the killing of any living being.

The scholar thought for a minute, then said, "Of course, how could I forget? I respect your beliefs, so if you will just hold the tiger's tail and loan me your staff, I'll kill it." So they exchanged places. But once he had the staff, the scholar started down the road with a jaunty step.

"Wait a minute," cried the priest. "Where are you going? Come back here and kill this tiger!"

"Oh, no," the scholar replied. "You have convinced me that it would be wrong to kill any living thing."

And with that, he took off down the road. The priest may still be holding that tiger's tail till this very day.

Traditional Korean dance.

Chapter V:
MAJOR RELIGIONS

According to 1982 estimates, Korea has some 60 million people, 40 million in southern Korea and 20 million in northern Korea. For more than 4000 years, the Korean people have maintained a unique Korean identity. Despite outside threats and internal conflicts, they have not only survived but have developed a strong national character consistent with a common cultural heritage. When someone asked Dr. George Paik, who then was the president of Yonsei University in Seoul, what the great accomplishment of Koreans was, Dr. Paik replied, "Why, perhaps it is simply that after four thousand years we are still Korean!"

The development of a Korean identity and the manifestations of a national character, through which Korea has been united, are rooted in the influence of religions of the past and present.

Four major religions, beside Christianity, have played major roles in molding Korean culture and in setting the historical direction. Three are the traditonal religions of Confucianism, Buddhism and Shamanism. The fourth is a relatively new religion called Ch'ondogyo, the "Teaching of the Heavenly Way," also known as "Tonghak." Among these religions, only Chundokyo and Shamanism emerged from within Korea. Buddhism and Confucianism originated elsewhere.

Buddhism and Confucianism, in particular, are intimately related to the rise and fall of kingdoms and dynasties and the tumultuous political life of the Korean people.

Religious conflicts have been a significant part of Korean political history. This fact emerged early and continues in the deep labyrinth of religious culture even today.

The myths and legends, like the ones preceding this chapter, are told over and over by Koreans, handed down from one generation to the next. They illustrate the way the traditional mind dealt with the basic questions of life, death, suffering and joy. They give clues to how pre-modern people explained existence before birth and after life. Many of the favorite folk stories have also integrated religious figures to such an extent that they are almost mythical.

Many present-day Koreans would say that the rise of science and the use of modern technology have wiped out the influence of old thought patterns. It is interesting to consider how true that is.

Imagine walking along a mountain path with a friend. At a turn in the trail, a stream cascades down through the rocks. On one of the larger boulders there is a small pile of stones and the friend carelessly picks up a stone and throws it over on the pile. Both stand and stare at the water and the rocks for awhile and then walk on, continuing the conversation. What has happened?

Without conscious thought, the so-called modern friend, trained in one of Korea's best universities and sent abroad for advanced study, has just made an offering to the spirits residing in the rocks and the mountain stream. The powerful belief that all things are infused with spirit is so pervasive that it has slipped into the Korean unconscious mind. That is why to this day, Shamanism, the true folk religion of Korea, retains such a powerful hold.

SHAMANISM

Shamanism stems from pre-literate societies and lacks a systematically expressed doctrine. Shamanism is difficult not only to understand but also to isolate from other religions. Moreover, because of its very nature, it has borrowed from others and tended to change in different times and places. Because of its adaptability Shamanism has also become part of other religions. There is disagreement about what the earliest religion was in Korea. Some believe it was religion which worshipped (or respected) "heaven." Others believe it was the spirit-worship now called Shamanism. Still others believe the two are inseparable.

Shamanism believes in a universe in which not only human beings, but animals and inanimate things also have souls or spirit. Above all spirits stands "Hananim", the "one spirit." Hananim seems to dominate the lives of the Korean people, for the name is continually on their lips. Curiously, however, they never really seem to actually worship "hananim." Koreans believe that Hananim, the creator, remains remote from the events of the world and rules the world through powers delegated to lesser gods.

Shamanism believes in a three-layer universe. In the upper layer, the bright world above heaven, live Hananim and the benevolent spirits. The present world where people and all animate and inanimate things live constitutes the middle layer. In hell, the lower layer, live all the evil spirits which are responsible for misfortune in the world. It is said that a person, after this present life, will either ascend to the upper level or descend to the lower one. Koreans seem to take immortality of some sort for granted. The later form of Buddhism has helped to give more content and meaning to this belief. Most Koreans also naturally accept the belief that everyone goes ultimately to Jeuh Seung, the future world after this world, and to King Ymna, the King of Judgment. Both of these have now become Buddhist terms as well, but they and many other ideas in Korean Buddhism represent a much older tradition and probably antedate Buddhism.

Shamanism may be the most pervasive religion in Korea. It has penetrated deeply into the custom and the culture of the Korean minjung. Nevertheless, any attempt to pin it down is in vain. It has no particular set location for worship and no particular doctrine. It may be practiced in one's residence, either inside the house or in the courtyard. It may also be practiced in public places, under the elm tree that stands either on the road leading to a village or in the middle of a village.

The practice of Shamanism takes the form of the "Kut." The Kut is performed by a Mudang. To com-prehend what Shamanism is one must gain an understanding of the Mudang and the Kut, for these two constitute the essence of Shamanism.

The Mudang   The Mudang may be called the priestess of Korean Shamanism for a Mudang is usually a woman, although there are male shamans. The Mudang's dance, her music and words constitute what Shamanism is. There are no scripture and no written documents. Korean Shamanism neither knows its founder, nor does it have leaders. It exists in and through the Mudang and is centered solely upon her.

How does one become a Mudang? One becomes a Mudang by inheriting the tradition and by learning the orthodox ritual preserved through many generations. One can become a Mudang through divine inspiration or "spirit illness" (Shinbyung). There is no set pattern of education, standard of examination or ordination process, although there is an initiation ritual.

The initiate goes through a trying period or "spirit illness." In external appearance, it is a form of mental illness, hysteria, or psychosomatic disorder. A woman who has "entered into the gods," "upon whom the gods have descended," or who is "possessed by gods" has hallucinations, dreams about mountain spirits or soldier spirits on horseback. She must have a ceremony of exorcism performed by a senior Mudang, following which she herself begins to dance in the "Kut." After this, the new Mudang performs an initiation Kut, inviting the gods to complete their descent and permit their chosen one to dance and sing as a Mudang.

Kut Ritual   The ritual the Mudang performs to appease the spirits or repel the spirits is called a "Kut." There are three kinds of Kut. The first is "Tangkut," which is performed to ask protection or blessing for an entire village or community. The second type, "Shinkut," is for the Mudang herself. It can be an initiation for a new Mudang or semi-annual prayer thanksgiving to the gods for their goodness and kindness. The third kind is the "regular Kut" performed for a living person to bring good fortune, to heal or to overcome misfortune. This ceremony can also be for a deceased person, asking that the spirit find rest in a pleasant place.

The ritual of a Kut may be divided into the following major five steps, although it is very difficult to distinguish the steps because there is no standardized procedure. The first step is a prelude. It is a rite of purification.

The second step is an invitation to the gods to descend. The Mudang sings and dances slowly with a staggered beat of the drum at the beginning. As the Mudang enters her trance, the beat of the music becomes faster and faster and the Mudang jumps higher and higher. During this ecstatic jumping dance, the spirits descend upon her and possess her body.

In the third step, the Mudang "plays" with the spirits through songs and different dances. This is to please the spirits which have descended. The fourth step is listening to the will or wish of the spirits. In between the songs and dances, the Mudang transmits the messages of the spirits to the participants.

The final, fifth step is the postlude, in which the Mudang will sing and dance briefly, praising the good and generous spirits. With this step, the Mudang will come out of the trance and return to a normal state.

History of Shamanism In early Korean history, Shaman practice was dominated by male Shamans called Barksoo. However, when Confucianism became the state religion male shamans gradually disappeared and female shamans took over the role. Around the end of the '70s, it was estimated that there were 100,000 Mudangs in Korea. The Daehan Chungdo Hae (Korean Mudang Association) has 63,000 registered members. Counting only the registered members, there is one Mudang for every 635 people in Korea. This is a high ratio. According to 1982 statistics there are some 35,000 Protestant ministers and 20,755 Buddhist monks. This means one Protestant minister for every 1,143 people and one Buddhist monk for every 2,000 people in Korea. This brief comparison reflects how shamanism is deeply rooted in the life of the Korean people.

Shamanism in Korea has traditionally been despised by Confucian intellectuals and persecuted by Confucian officials. Japanese colonial power in the name of modernization attempted to erase any shamanistic elements from Korean life. When Western Christian missionaries came to Korea, they attacked Shamanism. The Christian church still urges people to convert from Shamanistic practice. In spite of all these efforts to suppress it, the tie between the minjung and shamanism has increased.

Religion of Han Korean Shamanism can be called the religion of han. Korean women with all their problems are major clients of the Mudangs. The Mudang, through exorcism and appeasing the spirit, gives the han-ridden woman consolation and blessing. When poor people are sick, they feel there is no other way than the Mudang way to cure the sickness. The Mudang comes to them with a spirit of deep empathy and listens with understanding to their sad stories, shares their pains, and performs a "kut" for them. The Mudang tells them what to do to rectify past mistakes and mediates between them and the spirits. The person gains a sense of forgiveness and release. Now they can start a new life.

Moon Tong Hwan, a minjung theologian of Korea, assesses the role of the Mudang as follows:

"As the messiah is expected to come from the bottom, a Mudang comes from there whence the han-ridden minjung are crying. As with the prostitutes and the butchers, the profession of mudang is among the lowest. Furthermore, a true mudang has had in her past the bitter experience of han, and has gone through the death-resurrection experience. . . . Because of these experiences, she has a tremendous ability to empathize with the inner agonies of the han-ridden minjung and create around her a community of real trust. She is always an understanding friend to the minjung and at the same time a spiritual leader who can tell them the cause of their troubles and what remedies they should take. She functions as a Mudang upon the basis of this trusting Koinaia."[1]

Shamanism does not contain any moral teaching. No action guide is given to oppressed people to be liberated. Through the ritual of the Kut, they are released from the sense of pressure and assured help from the spirit.

In conclusion, the basic religion of Korean is Shamanism. The basic religious character of Korea and a Korean person is Shamanistic. For a Korean, the intellectual and ethical needs are met by Confucianism, the devotional life is fulfilled by Buddhism, but the heart, feeling and intuition are controlled by Shamanism. An observation made by an early missionary is still relevant. Homer B. Hulbert, who wrote a book of Korean history in 1907, said, "As a general thing, we may say that a Korean will be a Confucianist when in society, a Buddhist when he (or she) philosophizes and a spirit worshipper when he (or she) is in trouble … the underlying religion of the Koreans, the foundation upon which all else is more superstructure, is his (or her) worship."[2]

Even today it is safe to say that Shamanism, the original ethos of the Korean people, remains their basic instinct.

BUDDHISM

Buddhism was the first major world religion to come to Korea, introduced in 372 A.D., during the period of the Three Kingdoms. An Indian priest named Sundo brought scriptures and statues into Koguryu, the northernmost part of Korea. Only 20 years later, Kokookyang wang (King Kokookyang) ordered the entire nation to follow Buddhist teaching and seek blessings from Buddha.

The Kingdom of Paek'che, located in the southwest of Korea, received the new religion through another Indian priest, Maranata, who came through China in 384 A.D. One year after the Kingdom accepted Buddhism, a major temple was built in the capital. But in the south, the Kingdom of Silla was reluctant to embrace Buddhism. It was the most stable of the three Kingdoms and the ruling class was in firm control. They felt no need to bring in a new religion. The first Buddhist priest to enter that kingdom was a Koguryu priest named Mookhaja, who came south sometime around 417 A.D. Strong resistance against Buddhist teaching was manifested in the martyrdom, in 528 A.D. of Ichadon (Pak Yamchok), another priest.

Korean Buddhism comes from the Mahayana Buddhism that flourished in northeastern Asia, primarily in China. The Sun (Zen) sect was introduced to Korea during the later part of the Unified Silla (779-935). The Kyo Buddhist sect was exclusively concerned with the teaching of scriptures and doctrines. The Pure Land and Tontrie Buddhism as well as indigenized versions were popular among the common people.

Two Functions Korean Buddhism has had two primary functions, both of them connected with miracle-working. The first function is to bring health and wealth to an individual. The second is to bring national prosperity and security. It fit in easily with the popular beliefs and Shamanistic customs of the time. For the ruling class, Buddhism was an occult power that could defend the country from all evils, external or internal. For the minjung, Buddhism represented true life and future hope.

There was a bitter warfare between Buddhism and Confucianism when Confucianism was first taught. People who believed in Buddhism, the official religion, showed no mercy to Confucianists. In 1392, Koryu fell, and the situation was reversed. The Confucianists came into power and they showed no mercy to the Buddhists.

The Yi dynasty regarded the previous connection with Buddhism as disastrous and began almost immediately to curb its power. It moved the capital from Songdo to Seoul to escape the Buddhist environment. In 1397, the King confiscated many monasteries and in 1400 ended the formal reading of Buddhist scriptures in the palace. By 1422 the previous 13 Buddhist sects had been merged into only two: the Sun (or Zen) Buddhism and the Kyo (or "Pure Land") Buddhism.

During the Yi dynasty, Buddhism was driven into the hills and its priests cut off from the life of the cities. But it assumed shamanistic forms and penetrated deeply into the lives of the common people. Privilege and power had corrupted its original mission, but the shamanistic "cloak" that it put on in the mountains, kept its influence alive.

A Summary of the Teachings of Buddhism The origin is found in the teaching of Shiddhartha Gautama, Sakyammuni, who was born in northeastern India six centuries before Christ. He was born into a royal family but at the age of 29, he left home. Along with five friends he sought for a way to overcome human suffering. After awhile, he departed from his colleagues and went on his own way searching for truth. One day he attained the great enlightenment under the Buddhi tree at Buddh-Goya. He was 35 years of age.

The fundamental teaching of Buddhism lies in the "Four Precious Truths" which he expounded to his original five ascetic colleagues at Isipatana. The Four Precious Truths are: 1) Dukkha (Suffering), 2) Samudoya (The cause or origin of suffering), 3) Nirodha (The suppression of suffering), and 4) Magga (The way out of suffering).

Suffering is a part of life, but can be overcome by extinguishing the desires of the self and its senses, leading to a state of enlightenment and peace.

The way to escape desire and the suffering it produces is to follow the "middle path," which is generally referred to as the Noble Eightfold Path: 1) Right understanding, 2) Right thought, 3) Right speech, 4) Right action, 5) Right livelihood, 6) Right effort, 7) Right mindfulness, 8) Right concentration.

The heart of the eightfold path is wisdom and compassion, leading to the condition called Nirvana.

"Pure Land" Buddhism, with its emphasis on the compassion of Buddhism, has been more popular in Korea than the Sun of Zen Buddhism. The main worship of Pure Land Buddhism is a prayer-offering to give homage to the Amita Buddha, the compassionate Buddha.

In spite of the differences between Sun and Pure Land Buddhism, many have attempted to unify the two. Even today, they may be practiced by one monk at the same temple, Pure Land stressing the power of the grace of Amita Buddha, while Sun Buddhism advocates meditation and self-discipline as a means to achieve enlightenment.

Pure Land Buddhism practices are quite easily co-opted by Shamanistic practice. This is evident in the design of Korean Buddhist temples which have three types of buildings. The largest building at the center of the temple ground is the meditation hall where Buddha statues are placed. A smaller building adjacent to the main hall is where the dead are remembered and prayed for. The smallest, almost hidden behind the other buildings in the temple ground, is for the seven star spirits, and this is what catches the Korean "soul."

Although Korean Buddhism has been shamanized, it retains the ideal that Maitreya Buddha will come to the world to save the suffering minjung at the end of salvation history. Maitreya Buddha is love and compassion and will lead the suffering people into the future messianic world. The Korean minjung are attracted because it gives meaning to their suffering.

CONFUCIANISM

Historically and in terms of long-range influence on Korea's religious life, Confucianism is perhaps the second most important influence, ranking immediately after Shamanism. Confucianism has played a decisive role in shaping the social and political forms of Korean culture.

Everyone agrees that Korean Confucianism came from China. But no one is really sure of when it came. The title "Confucianism" comes from the name of the great teacher, Confucius, romanized as "K'ung Tzu" ("Kong Ja," the Korean pronunciation). He was born in 551 B.C., but the ideas in Confucianism are much older than Confucius himself. Confucius was, as he acknowledged, a collector and transmitter of the teaching now called after him. Accordingly, some sources say that Confucianism came to Korea in 1122 B.C., 500 years before Confucius' birth. Although it is extremely difficult to pinpoint the exact date, it is probably safe to say that it came when Korea began to use the Chinese written characters.

A Confucian college was established in Koguryu, the first of the ancient states to become a kingdom (located along the Yalu River in the north) in 372 B.C. Wangin, a Confucian scholar was sent to Japan in 285 B.C. to teach Non-uh, the Confucian Analects. Thus

Koreans became transmitters of religion and culture to what is now Japan.

Whether Confucianism is a religion or a philosophical system is debated by many scholars. Some say it is only a system of ethics. Here, however, Confucianism is considered as a religion because it provides a value system, a moral code, a world view and a framework of meaning for people's lives.

From the first, Confucianism steadily increased in influence until it eventually became the official teaching of the Yi Dynasty (1392-1910). Thus to the end of the Yi Dynasty in 1910, one can describe Korea as being basically a Confucian society. To some degree, this is so even today.

Confucius Confucianism is best understood by looking briefly at who Confucius was and what his teachings were.

Confucius (Kong Ja) was born in 551 B.C. in the state of Ku in the southern part of the present Shantung province in eastern China. It is believed that he came from the royal family of Shang, the dynasty that came just before the Chou dynasty in which he was born. According to the first history of China's dynasties, completed around 86 B.C., Confucius, though of royal ancestry, was poor and lived humbly.

Along with other young men displaced out of the upper classes by changing circumstances, he became a teacher. They knew "the arts" of classical learning and formed a "middle" class between the peasants and the aristocracy of the time.

H. G. Creel describes Confucius' relation with the common people, the minjung, as:

". . . His own early struggles gave him a sympathy for the common people that never left him, and which has colored Confucianism ever since. He resolved that insofar as he could have an influence, every young man of ability, no matter how humble, should have opportunity. Later, he would declare that he had never turned away an aspiring student no matter how poor, and asserted that every youth should be treated with respect until he had a chance to prove himself. . . ."[4]

Confucius held the same idea when he talked about the nobility. Confucius said that nobility depends on the mind and the spirit, not the pedigree, and that a man's worth depends on what he is, not on who his grandfather was.[5]

It must be noted that Confucius was talking about men. A woman's place in Confucian thought was a secondary one. Women's lives had meaning in patterns of relationship to men: that is as daughter, wife or mother. While in theory, it had potential as a source of fulfillment for women as well as men, in practice Confucianism had a conservative influence on the role of women.

Confucius was an ambitious man. He wanted to do two things: he wanted a public position and he wanted to alleviate the human misery that resulted from personal misconduct and misuse of power. In order to fulfill his ambition, he devoted himself to studying all the available classics. He pulled ideas together and taught disciples who sought positions in government where they could put their wisdom into practice.

Though some records say Confucius once occupied a very high government position in the state of Lu, no concrete evidence is available to substantiate that claim. He travelled from one state to another, preaching his doctrine and advocating education as the way to political and social reform. He returned to the state of Lu as an old man and died in 479 B.C.

The Teachings The religion called by his name is based on the Six Classics. These are: 1) the "Yeuk" (Book of Changes), 2) the "Sik" (Book of Odes, or Poetry), 3) the "Suh" (Book of History), 4) the "Ye" (Book of Ritual or Rites), 5) the "A'k" (Music) and 6) the "Choon Choo" (Spring and Autumn Annals). However, Confucius' ideas are best known through the "Non Uh," or Confucian Analects, a collection of his scattered sayings compiled by his disciples. As mentioned above, Confucius modestly said that his thoughts were neither new nor original. He was a "transmitter and not an originator." (Analects, VII, 1) His aim was to uphold and preserve tradition, the "good things." However, in transmitting, he originated something new.

According to Confucius' teaching, the virtues of the individual are comprised of "In-Yi" which means "righteousness" or "human-heartedness." "In" consists in loving others. (Analects, XII, 22). "In" is the inward quality of a person. It is the substance of character. The one who loves others is able to perform his duties in society. Therefore, "In" is inward substance of a person while "Yi" is the outward substance of a virtuous person. "Yi" means the "oughtness" of a situation. It is a categorical imperative. For instance, a father acts according to the way a father who loves his son should act; the son acts according to the way a son who loves his father should act. If one acts out of desire for "li" (profit or gain), then even though one does the right thing, one's action is not righteous or virtuous.

Confucius also taught that "If my principles are to prevail in the world, it is destiny. If they are to fall to the ground, it is destiny." In Korean, destiny or fate is translated "chun myung." Confucius described fate as the "Decree (Will) of Heaven," which he understood to include the forces of the whole universe. Thus to know "chun myung" is to acknowledge the inevitability of the world as it exists and to disregard external success or failure. When a person understands and accepts this, "In," the inner substance of human virtue, and "Yi," the outward substance of human virtue, are joined. Such a person is in harmony with heaven and fulfills his nature.

The principle which forms the basis of social relations is "Yeh," propriety. It is the basis of the code of proper conduct. This principle undergirds all basic human relationships: king and subject, father and son, husband and wife, old and young, friend and friend. When applied in human relationships, "Yeh" takes the form of family piety and of loyalty to the King. These are the foundation from which all virtues spring and in which all moral principles are rooted.

The person who acts according to "Yeh" is a superior person. It does not just happen. It takes time and discipline. Confucius, with regard to his own spiritual development, said, "At fifteen I set my heart on learning. At thirty I could stand. At forty I had no doubts. At fifty I knew the Decree of Heaven. At sixty I was already obedient to this Decree. At seventy I could follow the desires of my mind without overstepping the boundaries of what is right." (Analects, II, 4) In summary, what Confucius aimed at was to develop a superior person who disciplines himself, leads his family or rules the nation in harmony and peace.

Korean Confucianism Korean Confucianism emerged in the public spotlight during the late Koryu Dynasty when corruption was spreading in Buddhism, the state religion. During the period of King Songjong (981-997), a department of Confucian education was instituted and Confucian education was greatly encouraged. By 958, the National Examination System was instituted for civil services. At this time, Confucianism served not as a religion — Buddhism had center stage on that — but as a springboard for many individuals into civil service.

From the late 13th century and the early 14th century, however, the school of Neo-Confucianism began to provide a strong argument against Buddhism and a practical policy guide for land and currency reform. Popular resistance against corrupt Koryu officials and corrupt priests mounted. Confucianism rose in favor as its followers challenged the government.

The once great Koryu dynasty was now completely corrupt and Buddhism was steeped in this corruption. Confucian scholars were regarded as allies by the political groups who sought change. One such alliance was between the scholar Chung Mongju and the general Yi Sungkye who joined in the revolt that overthrew the dynasty.

Yi went on to become the first king of the new dynasty. Chung, faithful to his own teaching, was assassinated by opponents among the Confucianists because he could not bring himself to turn against the former king. The martyred Chung Mongju became the model of Confucian wisdom and virtue in Korea, while those who killed him lost the respect of the people.

One of the first acts of the new king was to establish a Confucian school. Called the Song-gyun-kwan, the school became the cornerstone of education in the new national teaching. It survives today as a major university where Confucianism is still taught and studied, though somewhat disregarded in the modern era.

Confucianism at its best has spoken to both the abstract and the practical concerns of the Korean people. Its debates over the meaning of human life and the universe have dealt with the relationship of mind ("Yi") to matter ("Ki") and in the practical world, of righteousness ("li") to profit or gain.

The tide of debate has washed back and forth, with high points where scholars with deep concern for the suffering of the nation produced practical solutions to educational, legal, economic and agricultural problems. There were also low points where they busied themselves with pointless arguments, upholding the status quo.

At their best, they paid attention to the common people. Many of the strongly held views of Koreans today come from teachings based on concern for the poor. One of the best known of the reform teachers is Chung, Yak Yong (1762-1836). He wrote, "The people today know nothing of peace because of fear, anxiety and anguish. No one cares about the people while they are fainting out of hunger. . . . I wept again and again as I saw their misery."[5]

He taught that politics must be carried out for the people and must work to make the people equal. Thus rulers exist for the people and not the opposite.

He used the following story to make his point.

"Once upon a time there was only the people, no rulers. The people lived together, and when they had a fight over something, they couldn't judge who was right or wrong. There was an elder who could understand justice a little better, so they went to him and asked him to judge. Everyone obeyed his decisions and asked him to be their ruler."[6]

From this simple story, Chung's principle is clear that rulers emerge from the people to guide and serve. This implies that people are the active subjects of their own history. Such social ideas derived from Confucian thought have been strong antidotes to oppression.

But like Buddhism before it, Confucianism became weak when it got too close to the comfort of those in the seats of power. Too closely identified with the ruling power, its lights dimmed when those of the Yi dynasty went out in 1910.

CH'ONDOGYO — THE TEACHING OF THE HEAVENLY WAY

Among all the religions Korea has known, none has made a more drastic and concrete impact on the nation and on the life of its people than has Ch'ondogyo. It brought down the long-lived and well-established feudalism and ushered in an era of equality and justice. Ch'ondokyo mustered people:

— to revolt against the internal corruption of the Yi dynasty's political practice, social injustice and discrimination,

— to stand up against foreign powers that wanted to dominate Korea, and

— to oppose all other religions, particularly foreign ones such as Christianity.

It advocated a new humanity, a new society and a new world.

Ch'ondogyo emerged in the middle of the 19th century and was firmly established by the end of the 19th century when Korea was going through the most crucial point of its modern history. The feudalistic society grounded in the philosophy and ethics of Confucianism began to suffer greatly from corruption, misuse of power and factionalism among the royal families and the ruling class (Yangban).

Externally, Japan had forced the opening of the ports of the "Hermit Kingdom" in 1876 and the Treaty of Amity and Commerce between Korea and the United States had been signed. Korea became a pawn of the big powers. The downfall of the dynasty, the disintegration of society and collapse of the nation were imminent.

The Founder The founder of Ch'ondogyo was Ch'oe Cheu (1824-1863), born as an illegitimate child of a well- known Confucian scholar. The early death of his parents and his social status meant that he would not be able to have a respectable position in either society or government. His own fate awakened him to the sickness of his society. In order to see the reality of social conditions, he traveled all over the country and recorded the following:

"Our country is full of evildoers, and so people cannot have a peaceful day throughout the four seasons. This is harmful destiny. We hear that the Western powers win whenever they fight, and gain whenever they attack, and that there is nothing that they cannot do. If the whole world were destroyed, there would be lamentation that would burst lips. Where will peace for the people come from?"[7]

Everywhere he went, he saw people acting only out of self-interest, violating the principle of heaven. So the total destruction of the people and nation was clearly predictable.

Seeking some way to uphold and teach the way of Heaven, he visited various religious groups and examined all existing religions in Korea, including Roman Catholicism. But he became convinced that neither Buddhism nor Confucianism could bring salvation to his nation and people. They were religions, but they were only partial answers. At this point, he determined to make a new religion that would liberate the minjung from their suffering and save the nation.

After agonizing, inner turmoil and a strange religious experience during a seven-month meditation, he finally arrived at the Realization of Ch'ondo (the Heavenly Way) in the early morning of April 5, 1860. This is the beginning of Ch'ondogyo. It was first known as Tonhak (Eastern Learning) in contrast to Seuhak (Western Learning), the name given to Roman Catholicism.

The basic doctrine of Ch'ondogyo is found in this formula of twenty-one words used as a chant:
"Chigi Kumji Wonwi Taegang.
Si Ch'onju chohwa Cong.
Yonse Palmang Mansaju."
This can best be translated as "Infinite (Being) now within me, I yearn that you may flow into all living beings and created things. Wait on God, Master of creation. Forget not God. All things are done and known through God." In order to hold to this formula, the condition of "Soosim Cheunggi" — making right the heart, putting straight the soul — is required.

In this doctrine, the central concept is "Si Ch'onju." Ch'onju literally means "the Lord of Heaven." It is quite different from the Confucian notion of the principle of Heaven. In Ch'ondogyo, the Lord of Heaven is God who is absolute, transcendant, the infinite and supreme Being. The main duty is to wait on, work for, and bear God. Ch'oe established this credo because he believed that the seed or substance of Heaven is implanted in every person.

Ch'oe was suspected by the government on two counts. One, he preached a dangerous doctrine which they said agitated ignorant people to overthrow the existing order. Secondly, he used the same term to describe God as the Roman Catholic Church used. At that time preaching the Roman Catholic doctrine was against the law. The term was Ch'onju. He was arrested along with 33 of his followers on November 20, 1863, and was beheaded at Taegu on March 10, 1864.

A Pro-Korean Faith Ch'oe has often been described as anti-Western when in fact, he was simply pro-Korean. He sought answers to Korea's social problems out of Korean experience. He was a champion of Korea's urban poor and her farmers. They followed him because he stressed Korean initiative. They knew he trusted in them.

Ch'oe, Haewal took up the leadership of Ch'ondogyo and led it for 35 years after the founder's martyrdom. He stressed a person's essential oneness with God and developed the doctrine of "in nae ch'on," or "heaven inside."

A person does not just serve or wait on God. A person is God. He asked, "Where is mind (person)? It is in Heaven. Where is Heaven? It is in the mind. Outside mind there is no Heaven, and outside Heaven there is no mind. Therefore, Heaven and mind are not two things."[8]

Since a person is essentially one with God, relationships between persons must reflect this reality. Since one's fellow person is divine, one has to treat the fellow person with utmost concern, respect, and sincerity. This human relationship is summarized in the doctrine of "Sain yoch'on" — treat a person as you treat God — which was developed subsequently.

Ch'ondogyo taught the following: Serve all persons like God. Do not strike a child, for striking a child is striking God. Respect all persons in the house like God. Particularly, respect your daughter-in-law like God. God never judges others. Therefore judging others is judging God.[9]

The following story is told as an illustration of this teaching.

Ch'oe, Haewal, while once visiting So Taeksun, one of his disciples, heard someone weaving cloth. He questioned his disciple to test him. "Who is weaving in your house?" So answered, "My daughter-in-law is weaving." Then Ch'oe said with authority, "No! God is weaving the cloth."[10]

The concept of a person's essential divinity and the principle of "Sain yoch'on" was a revolutionary idea in the feudalistic society and a dynamic counter against the ethical system of Confucianism. It was particularly liberating for women.

Another important doctrine of Ch'ondogyo concerns evil. Ch'ondogyo rarely uses the term "sin." It prefers to use the term "disease" or "sickness" to describe personal wrong-doing and collective wrong-doing.

"Disease" or "sickness" is abnormal in a person's mind, in relationships between persons and in social life as a whole. As physical sickness kills the person, this spiritual "sickness" destroys life, community and nation. Ch'ondogyo takes the nature of evil in human society quite seriously. Ch'ondogyo also teaches that the Kingdom of Heaven can come on earth and that cooperation is the way to bring good.

A Revolutionary Religion In essence, Ch'ondogyo was a revolutionary religion. It contained the seed of nationalism, awakening the mind of the common people to the idea of equality and justice. These ideas are easily convertible into political ideas. The growth of Ch'ondogyo made it a social movement of major importance in the modern history of Korea.

In May 1893, more than 20,000 Ch'ondogyo believers assembled carrying banners saying, "Reject Japan and Repel the Foreigners." It was an appeal to the government to stand firm in the face of foreign powers, particularly the Japanese. It was based on the belief that foreign influence was the root cause of personal and social "disease."

The Korean government, however, no longer had either the will nor the power to resist the foreign powers. When the Ch'ondogyo followers saw the impotence of the government, the movement moved into the second stage. It began a violent struggle against sterile government and corrupt rulers. In February 1894, there was an uprising in Cholla Province which demanded correction of unfair and unjust taxation. More than a thousand people, mostly farmers and laborers, attacked the provincial offices and punished the officials. They distributed the grains collected as taxes and raided the arms depot. This was followed by revolts in several places. The people had taken matters into their own hands.

Unbelievably, the weak government requested the military assistance of the Chinese in order to suppress their own people. The Chinese troops arrived at Asan Bay on June 8, 1894. This action gave the Japanese an excuse for sending in their troops. This encounter led to the Sino-Japanese War of 1894. Ironically, the Tonghak Rebellion, subdued finally by the Korean government with the assistance of these foreign powers, helped the Japanese to realize their long held dreams of occupying Korea.

Although the Tonghak revolt failed as a revolution, it made a significant impact on Korea. It quickened the modernization that was beginning to develop and heightened the national consciousness of the Korean people. This later culminated in the nationalistic Independence Movement of 1919 against Japanese occupation.

Practice Today The Ch'ondogyo religion still has many followers, although it has suffered from the division of Korea. Before 1945, most of its adherents were in the northern part of the country. The central headquarters is located in Seoul. It has active associations, preaching halls and branches all over southern Korea. Ch'ondogyo has overseas branches and there are several minor sects which have come out of the original Tonghak movement.

The obligations of this belief center around prayer and rituals. The believer practices a form of silent prayer, informing God before and after any action of what is happening. The five rituals are:

1) chanting the Ch'ondogyo prayer mentioned earlier to purify the heart;
2) making an offering of a bowl of clean water;
3) dedicating a spoonful of uncooked rice at each meal to God and collecting it each month to take to Church;
4) gathering with family and other believers on a regular basis for prayer; and,
5) individual prayer.

NOTES

1. Moon, Tong Hwan, "Korean Minjung Theology: An Introduction," unpublished paper, January 1982.

2. Homer B. Hulbert, *The Passing of Korea*, Seoul, Yonsei University Press, 1969, first published in 1906, pp. 403-404.

3. H.G. Creel, *Confucius and the Chinese Way*, Harper and Row, New York, 1949, p. 26.

4. Ibid, pp. 44-45.

5. Korean Cultural History, II, 1. "The History of Korean Political Ideas" by Kim, Dooyoung, p. 112.

6. Wonmok: *The Original Shopper*, by Chung, Yakyong.

7. "P'odongmun," Ch'ondogyo Kyongjon, or "Declaration," Ch'ondogyo Scripture, p. 5.

8. Ch'oe, Haewal, "Ch'on, In, Kwisin, Umyang" (Heaven, Man, Ghost, Yin Yang), Ch'ondogyo Kyongjon, p. 144.

9. Ch'oe, Haewal, "Naesudomun" (Writing on the Religion of Moral Exercise in the Home), Ch'ondogyo Kyongjon, pp. 239-240.

10. Paek, Se-myong, Tonghak Sasang Kwa Chon-dogyo, (Tonghak Thought and Ch'ondogyo), Seoul, Tonghaksa, 1956, p. 125.

QUESTIONS

1. What human needs are fulfilled by religious belief?

2. Is it possible to separate religion from the other points of human life? What do you think are some good results from religion being in all of life? Are there bad results?

3. From reading this chapter, how do you think Koreans feel about religion?

4. Are there customs or practices in this country which could be described as "shamanistic?"

5. Is there any difference between how Korea's ruling groups used religion and the role religion played in the lives of ordinary people? Do you see any parallels in this country?

Modern Korean art which still uses some of the ancient symbols.

CHO, WHA SOON:
A MODERN APOSTLE

The guard pushed her into the cold, lonely cell and the iron door clanged shut behind her. She was tired, angry and confused. The workers needed her badly, many had been fired and had no place to go. Their struggle seemed to be at its height. Yet here she was, plucked from among them and thrust into solitary confinement, in a prison hundreds of miles from home. She sank to the floor as the question rose from her lips, "God why? Why now? What is the meaning of my being put in prison now? What are you trying to tell me?"

It really seemed a fluke, a mistake, that the Rev. Cho, Wha Soon was in prison at this particular time. She had just been through some of the most tension-filled weeks in her whole history as minister of the Inchon Urban Industrial Mission. Yet through all the confrontations with the police, and even the terrible beating she experienced at their hands after a recent prayer meeting, still she had not been arrested. Then, while she was in Pusan to attend the trial of some of the workers there, she attended a prayer meeting for those recently imprisoned set up by some of the Pusan ministers. When she arrived at the church, she was immediately approached by one of the ministers in charge, who nearly begged her to be the speaker at the meeting that night. All the others who had been slated to participate were being kept under house arrest and there was no one to speak to the crowd that had assembled.

Rev. Cho was completely taken aback, but finally, reluctantly, she agreed to say a few words. She proceeded to tell the audience about the Dong-il Textile Company laborers' problem in Inchon. Though participation in prayer meetings in Seoul did not usually bring such harsh retaliation, it was obvious, after she began talking, that this was the first news that the people of Pusan had had of the Don-il Textile incident. The reaction of the police was much harsher.

Certainly, she never would have she would be arrested. That's exactly what had happened. It seemed completely untimely and she ached for the workers because her absence would be an added burden to them in their struggle. Only one thing was sure: her future, at this point, was unsure.

It was not the first time in her life that she had faced an uncertain future, nor the first time that she had been imprisoned. In fact, her life might be described as that kind of a journey — one that led to numerous dangerous and uncertain situations. But her goal and her commitment, formed in her early school days, never changed — that of helping her country and her people to rise out of poverty.

At the end of World War II, when Cho, Wha Soon was just beginning junior high school, Korea was largely a poor, rural society. Eighty percent of the people lived in the countryside. As did many other young people at that time, Cho wanted to devote her life to helping those in the countryside improve their lives. Even at this young age, the notion of contributing something to society was emerging in her mind.

It was in her local church that Cho, Wha Soon and some of her friends formed a group to seriously consider how they could someday go forth and contribute to the elimination of poverty in Korea. They met together regularly, read and discussed the Bible and prayed for their country. They also tried to discern what their roles should be in the future. The group together decided what fields of expertise they would need to help in the rural areas. Then they decided which of the group members should pursue what field of study or training. It was decided that Cho would go to medical school and become a doctor. She personally decided that she would forego marriage and children in order to carry out her work to the fullest extent.

By the time they were in high school, the group had dwindled down to only three girls who remained committed to their original goals. After high school, these three obtained teaching certificates and went to the rural area to work. In this way they would be contributing to the people in the country, they would learn firsthand what life was like and how to relate to the people there, and they would be earning a little money. They not only taught school, but they tried a variety of projects, mostly on an experimental basis. They raised pigs and chickens to help the people have a better diet. They started a church since there wasn't one in the area.

After two years there, Cho, Wha Soon came to one of the first big changes along the road of her journey. She wasn't one to go off alone very much, but one day she took a walk up into the mountain near the village. There she began to think about the things they had been doing in the village those past two years. She thought of how they had tried to help the people improve their standard of living. And it struck her that not only was there poverty in material goods, there was also poverty in spirit among the villagers. Then she realized that material development alone would be insufficient to help her nation escape from its poverty. The lack of hope and faith in the people were at least as crippling as the lack of material things. She had discovered that drinking by many of the rural people was quite excessive. They believed their lives to be so unstable that it was useless to prepare for anything in the future.

That day on the mountain it seemed that God was trying to tell Cho something. Suddenly it came to her — that she should go to seminary and become a minister! She was really quite surprised at this, for she had never considered such a role for herself, though her family had all converted to Christianity when she was still quite young. But the message seemed very clear to her that day.

So Cho, Wha Soon changed from the path of medicine to that of religion, and she took her first step on that path. She returned home and took the entrance examination to the Methodist Seminary in Seoul. She questioned her own wisdom at doing this and had

little hope of passing the exam because it had been two whole years since she had even looked at a book. So she was truly amazed when she learned that she had indeed passed, on the first try!

But now there was another problem — where to get the money for school fees. Up until high school, her family had been rather well-off. Her father owned and ran a transporting business with 10 horses. But then the Korean War broke out, the horses were stolen or killed. Overnight they had become destitute. Since then, all they had been able to do was eke out a living. So helping her with school fees was out of the question for Cho's family. She went to everyone she could think of for help, but, though they were sympathetic, no one had much money in those days.

Now, there were only a few days left before registration at the seminary. She began to wonder if this was really what God wanted her to do. She had discussed her predicament several times with one of her close friends, one of those who had gone to the country with her. Once again she went to her friend's house to unburden herself. Her friend, too, came from a family that was not wealthy. The father had been killed in the Korean War and she worked hard to help support the family and put her younger sisters and brothers through school.

That night Cho and her friend talked again about her desire to go to seminary and her purpose for doing so. At the end of their talk, her friend said to her, "Oh, just go on back home." Cho thought this rather strange, but again her friend said, "Just go on home." Still puzzled, she walked back home, and when she went inside, she discovered a white envelope on her desk. She opened it and found exactly enough money to cover her first semester in seminary.

Cho was moved to tears. She wondered how in the world her friend had been able to get that money together for her. She was so deeply touched by this act that even to this day she has never told her friend thanks. "It is one of those things where words can't express the depth of gratitude I feel toward her. We each know that the other knows, but it seems that putting it into words would break something very precious. Just being friends, I hope, is expression enough."

She did all kinds of jobs to pay her way and she studied hard. Before she could finish, she became ill and had to drop out for a year. When she finally finished seminary in 1963, she was already in her late twenties while all her classmates were much younger.

Her first assignment as a new seminary graduate

was not as an assistant to a minister of a thriving urban church where there are opportunities for further study and advancement. Instead, the bishop sent her to an isolated island off the coast of Inchon. She never asked any questions about where she was being sent. She was ready to go wherever God wanted. In fact, she didn't even know the name of the island or where it was located. She just went.

As soon as she stepped off the boat, all she could see in the village were small shacks, chicken droppings all over the place, and no roads. "It was like a place where nomads had encamped and just stayed on." These villagers were refugees from northern Korea and had escaped to the south about 13 years previously. "They weren't exactly poor. They ate well from the fish they caught and sold, from the food they raised, and from the chickens which were everywhere. But they didn't know how to save their money and prepare for the future or for their children's education. Also tuberculosis was somewhat of a problem, and they were quite superstitious."

Cho walked through the village and saw her church building high up on a hill. The windows were all broken out and the gate had fallen off its hinges. She walked inside the church. What she saw was the same as the rest of the village — chicken droppings and dust were the only congregation this church had had for the past five years. She asked a neighbor, "Are there any Christians around here?" The neighbor tossed a reply, "Ugh! If you mention Jesus Christ around here, all the people will run!"

Cho, Wha Soon could have returned to Seoul or Inchon and started a church there on her own. Or she could have changed her mind about being a pastor and started again to pursue a vocation in medicine. But she didn't. She stayed with a Christian elder in a nearby village and traveled everyday back and forth to her new church. She rolled up her sleeves and cleaned out the church singlehandedly.

The first Sunday was a cold December 19th, 1963. After some hesitation as to whether anyone would show up, she decided to go ahead and hold services. She rang the church bell that morning and went in to see if anyone had come. There was only one man present. She wondered what she should do and thought to herself, "They never told us in seminary what to do in a case like this?" But then she decided that even if there were only one person, God would want her to go ahead, so she preached her sermon to the lone listener, despite the cold wind blowing through the glassless windows.

She later learned that her solitary congregation member was a young man who had been shot in the head during the Korean War. His wound had caused permanent brain damage, but not enough to stop him from going all over the village announcing, "Hey, there is a beautiful young girl preaching in the church!"

The next service, which was Christmas eve, was attended by a much larger gathering — all men! It was winter and they couldn't go out on the sea to fish because of the cold. They had no movie theater or any other place to go for entertainment, so they came to the church to see the "beautiful young lady preacher." Since it was Christmas, Cho had gotten together some of the young children of the village, to present a special Christmas program. The men came into the church, rudely leaving their shoes on[1] and puffing on their cigarettes. She held the service anyway. Afterwards, the men went out and to add to their night's fun, they pelted the church with rocks. The rocks bounced and rolled off the corrugated tin roof producing a frightful noise, as Cho and the children crouched in a corner inside. After the men had had their "fun," she and the children left, too.

Despite such treatment, Cho did not give up. Instead, she returned to her home church in Inchon, got some financial help to buy cement and glass, and returned to the church to repair it. However, she couldn't find a single soul in the village who would help. So she said to herself, "By Jove, if that's the way they are going to be, I'll just do it myself!" And, though she'd never done anything like this before and didn't know where to start, she rolled up her sleeves and mixed cement, patched up cracks, put on wallpaper, and put in windows herself.

"It was sort of a half-baked job, but at least I got it done! I let the people know I was serious about staying, and it seemed that after this they began to have a new respect for me. Eventually I got to know a few of them. They were mostly mothers who, while taking care of their children, also dug for oysters. I would often help them dig."

Life in this village for Cho, Wha Soon was always full of varied experiences and incidents. Everyday she was learning more about their life and how to relate to these people. But her real test of faith came one day when she was asked to help a young girl who had gone insane. The girl just sat around all day never saying a word. The family had tried all the shamanistic rituals but with no luck. So the mother asked Cho to come and pray for her daughter. Cho said she would, but after agreeing, she realized that her whole ministry would be judged by the village people by whether or not she could cure this girl. With that realization, Cho's heart sank. She had real doubts about whether people could be healed by prayer or whether miracles like that could really happen today as they did in the Bible.

She stayed up all night pacing the floor and wringing her hands. Finally she began praying, though it was really more like a challenge to God. "God, now come on. Is it really possible to heal someone by praying? I admit I have my doubts. What am I going to do tomorrow at that girl's house?" On and on the conversation went, continuing throughout the night.

She could have made up an excuse and not gone to the family the next day, but she didn't. "When I first entered their home and saw the young girl, I felt so shaky and scared that I thought to myself, 'You aren't the patient. I am!'" Nevertheless, for five days she stayed with them praying, hardly eating or drinking anything. Finally the girl looked up at Cho and said something. She announced to her parents, "This evangelist's faith is the strongest of anybody here." That was the breakthrough, and after that the girl began to communicate again. It was as much a miracle to Cho as it was to the girl and her family.

After this, the people in the village became more friendly to her. Over a three-year period, she was able to communicate and get along quite well with the villagers who were at first so suspicious of her.

Another step along her journey was soon to take place, however. Korea was starting on its course to become one of the most rapidly industrialized countries in the world. The speed with which this had been done was quite upsetting to a society which had traditionally been agricultural. Farmers began to find it difficult to support their families. As their children got to be teenagers, more and more of them began going into the cities in hope of finding jobs. Many of these young people ended up in factories, not even making enough to sustain themselves, much less to send money to their families as they had hoped.

Because of this trend, Korea's population was beginning to shift. By 1966 already 25 percent were living in the urban areas. Ten years later, it was approaching 40 percent. As the numbers of laborers in the cities grew, many problems developed. It seemed that this was a segment of society in which the church should take a special interest.

In 1960, United Methodist missionary, George Ogle, organized Korean pastors and initiated a new form of mission called the Urban Industrial Mission (U.I.M.). It was lacated in Inchon. They soon discovered that they needed a female staff person because about one-third of the labor force was composed of young women, mostly from the countryside. The women worked at weaving machines and sewing machines, at microscopes assembling tiny electronic parts, and at other labor-intensive work.

The pastors went to Cho, Wha Soon to ask her to work with them in this new mission to laborers, but she refused. Though she didn't tell them, she later revealed, "I was suspicious of ministers and evangelists who did not pastor a church, but who worked in some organization or agency. Such people always seemed to be corrupt to me, or usually became that way after a while. Besides, I felt that God's will for ministers was to work in the pastorate. That's how conservative I was."

The U.I.M. men came back to Cho, Wha Soon several times, telling her what wonderful work the U.I.M. was, but she wasn't convinced. Finally, they went back to her once more and said, "Look, we can't find anyone else to do this kind of work and these young girls who come from the countryside need help in adjusting to urban life. You are the only female pastor we know. We need a female pastor in this U.I.M."

At that point she said, "Well, why didn't you say so in the first place? O.K., I'll do it." Cho, Wha Soon had always felt that she should do the work that no one else could to do. Her acceptance of this position at U.I.M. brought about many changes in her life and especially in her understanding of God's mission.

The training that one goes through in order to become a U.I.M. staff worker does not consist of lectures in a classroom, or logging hours in a seminar. The training is six months of actually becoming a laborer and working right alongside the others in a factory or other workplace.

For six months Cho, Wha Soon tasted the life of a worker, the way workers have to live it. She was assigned to work in the Dong-il Textile Factory. She was treated like any other worker right from the beginning. Indeed, at first no one knew that she was any different from anyone else. After applying for the job, she was kept waiting in the company office for several hours before being called. She was then sent to the kitchen to work. She went to the kitchen, but no one had explained to her what her duties were. She stood there for a minute until one of the other employees recognized her as a newcomer. "Hey, you!

Get over there and wash those dishes!" The words shouted at her came from a country-girl much younger than herself.

Anger flashed in Cho's cheeks. She was older than that girl and in Korea's Confucian society where age makes a difference, a younger person is supposed to address anyone older with respect. Cho, Wha Soon had been a preacher for the past few years. She had become accustomed to being addressed in "high talk" and treated with deference. But when she entered the factory as a worker, overnight she was knocked off her pedestal. She was now in a situation where someone younger could just say, "Hey, you!" and get away with it.

Out on the floor of the factory, she made rounds of the various departments, noting the long working days of the women who labored at noisy and hot machines and breathed cotton lint that filled the air. Once off work they went home to one dingy, airless little room, often used alternately by women on other shifts.

Salaries then averaged $20 a month (12 years later they were up to $60, though still well below the government figure of $100 a month — what it takes for a single person to live). The Rev. Cho observed that romantic ties came quickly and easily in such a setting, where there was little else to break the monotony. Emotional and physical tragedies often were the end product.[2]

At first, during Cho's six-month period of training, she thought her role was to get workers to attend church or perhaps to hold services for them in the factory someplace after working hours. But at the end of the week, after long, hard hours of physical labor she was unaccustomed to, she found that on Sunday, her only day off, she could not even raise her body out of bed. This really shocked her. She remembers thinking to herself, "Here I am, a minister of the church, and I can't even make myself get out of bed to attend Sunday services! How can I expect the other workers who are less motivated, to go on their only day of rest?!"

It was then that she first began to question her ideas of what it means to be a good Christian. Up until then, she had thought that going to church every Sunday was the central act and main responsibility of a Christian. Now all kinds of questions and doubts began enter her mind. Slowly she began to learn how the church and ministers appear to those in other walks of life, especially to those on the bottom rung of society. And she was ashamed by what she learned.

"During my six months of working as a laborer, I found that as soon as workers who had become my friends learned that I was a minister, our relationship became somewhat awkward. So later, I tried to keep my identity a secret, and worked to become friends with them. But when they did find out who I was, it was so surprising to them that a distance developed between us. They usually had somewhere in their minds that a minister is to be looked upon as a god, church is only a place for worship, and it is impossible for such lowly beings as themselves to become acquainted with a preacher.

"When I became aware of this, I was shocked and ashamed. I realized that the church, and we ministers, must become aware of this fact. I can understand why workers are so distant from the church when they see that the 'holy,' rich lives of ministers are so different from the life of Christ, who was a laborer himself."

After her training period in the factory, Cho joined the Inchon U.I.M. as a full-time staff member. The U.I.M. was feeling its way as to how it could best help the laborers, but they felt that their primary job was to hold services and teach the Bible to them. Soon, however, they began to learn from the workers themselves what was needed and how U.I.M. could really help them.

"One day about 15 workers, with whom I had become friends, met together and gave me an opportunity to talk freely with them. Mostly they wanted to talk about girl-boy problems. After that, they wanted to continue meeting. Eventually we selected a group name and a chairperson and proposed to do something formally. The format and content of that first formal meeting was like what we use in church services. However, at the next meeting, no one showed up. These workers later explained to me, 'We do not want to meet just so that you can get us to believe in Christ and increase your church membership. Therefore, we don't want anything to do with your meetings.' It was from that point on that I decided not to use a religious structure or form. I realized that I, a minister, had to truly be in their situation and live like them.

"Later, workers came to have an interest in the U.I.M. group activities that had been started, because they stressed concerns and needs the workers had, such as recreation, home economics, music, hobbies, etc. In this way, workers gradually became involved in our program.

"This was the first stage of our U.I.M. work, but we soon learned that these activities were only one way to help the workers, and it had its limitations. In order to find out what other needs they had, we began listening and dialoguing with them about their jobs and the problems they were facing at work. In doing this, the workers (and we) learned that one of their weaknesses was their own lack of awareness about how the factories were being run and what their rights were.

"This led to a second stage in our U.I.M. program in which we tried to help workers gradually come to an understanding of their human rights, the original nature of humanity, truth, love, and faith in God and Jesus. This understanding on the part of the workers led to the next stage of work. As the workers became more aware of their situation, they became interested in labor unions as one means of securing their rights and interests. For U.I.M. this meant carrying out labor education — discussion of the labor laws, laborers' rights and labor problems as they arose."

But it takes lots of inner strength and courage for young, uneducated workers to stand up for their rights against the big, rich, sophisticated company owners and managers. Cho, Wha Soon began to realize, as she had in the countryside, that faith in God was needed to provide the confidence, conviction, and hope that these women needed in their struggle for dignity. Faith would give them courage to say "no" instead of having to say "yes" to everything the company dished out.

This led to Bible study and worship which was really meaningful to the workers. They were not suspicious of Cho's motives now, because they knew she was trying to help them for their own sakes, not for some church record or to boost her own prestige as a minister. This was different; this was genuine. Many of the workers did come to believe, in their own time and for their own reasons.

During the months and years that followed, Cho began to see exciting things happen at U.I.M. She saw young, timid girls from the countryside become strong, articulate, confident young women, as they realized that they are worthy, acceptable beings. They realized that they, too, are made in the image of God who have the right and responsibility to stand up for themselves.

As the workers became more aware and spiritually strong, they began to demand that they be treated more humanely on the job. They demanded that they stop being beaten, they stop being forced to work 14 or 15 hours a day against their wills, and they stop being forced to give sexual favors to foremen and managers in order to collect their pay.

This led to demonstrations and protests, arrests and interrogations by the police. The police were surprised to meet young women who knew about their legal and human rights and they wanted to know where they had gotten these notions and information. The workers were afraid to get Rev. Cho or the U.I.M. in trouble. But harsh treatment and beatings by the police or KCIA forced the young women to tell where they had studied and who had taught them. As a result, over the years, Cho, Wha Soon has been picked up and questioned by the authorities some 300 times. Once she was held three months in prison, supposedly for a sermon she preached at a workers' picnic, though no charges were ever brought against her.

Over the years, Cho, Wha Soon has maintained contact with her friends at the Dong-il Textile Factory where she did her six months training. In this factory she discovered that there were 1,100 women and only 200 men workers. However, the men were in control of the union, despite the fact that the lion's share of the union dues came from the women. After these facts were made known to the women, they became angered at how they were being manipulated. Finally they succeeded in electing the first female chairperson, Lee, Chong Gak, of a union with over 1,000 members. Later nine other unions of over 1,000 members elected female chairpersons, though these groups had no connection with U.I.M.

A jump from 0 to 10 female union leaders seemed to alarm the powers-that-be, but for some reason the pressure was brought to bear primarily against the Dong-il Textile workers. Cho, Wha Soon was also falsely accused of being a communist. The authorities, in a male-dominated Confucian society, seemed to find it unbearable when women took action against being treated as second-class citizens.

But threats and harrassment against the workers did not dampen their spirits. When it came time for another union election on February 20, 1978, it was almost certain that the women at Dong-il would again elect a chairperson from among themselves. On the day of the election, however, the room was broken into by 30 men carrying buckets of human feces. Wearing rubber gloves, they dumped the contents of their buckets all over the room and the workers, rubbing it in their eyes, ears, noses and mouths, pulled their hair, tore their clothing and ruined the ballots. In addition, all 124 of these workers were fired and the male chairperson of the government-controlled Federation of Korean Trade Unions (F.K.T.U.) circulated their names to all the other companies, effectively blacklisting them from being hired somewhere else.

If the authorities thought this action would silence the workers, they were sadly mistaken. In the weeks that followed, they held demonstrations, protested with hunger fasts, publicized their situation by distributing leaflets and even tried to get the attention of the government-censored mass media. Of course, they also told their stories at prayer meetings, and it was at one of these, on September 22, 1978, that the workers, Rev. Cho and others who attended the service, were badly beaten by plainclothesmen and held in custody for days afterward.

Though the workers themselves come to their own decisions about what actions they will take and in what ways they will work to solve their problems, Rev. Cho always feels a special responsibility for them and the call to be with them in their suffering. After the women were fired, many of them had no place to go and nothing to eat, so she housed as many as she could in the U.I.M. office, feeding them noodles from her own meager salary, and literally giving them the clothes off her back.

Despite their treatment by the authorities, and the many obstacles that are constantly placed before them, the U.I.M. and especially Cho, Wha Soon's role in it, have had a real impact and have yielded much fruit. But there is so much more to be done, and so few who are willing to help, that Rev. Cho is convinced she must continue to do what she can. Of course, the work is both physically and emotionally exhausting. She says she constantly feels a need to read and study more and to spend more time in prayer. But there always seems to be a crisis or an urgent problem with laborers at one factory or another. So she never seems to have the time or energy to pick up a book or even to pray.

During the Dong-il Textile workers' struggle, Cho realized that she had been working in U.I.M. for 12 years. She remembered back when she first joined the U.I.M. staff. George Ogle had said then that an organization becomes hard to change when the person in charge heads it for more than 10 years. So Cho began to wonder if she shouldn't step aside and find someone else to take over the Inchon U.I.M. work. She was certainly tired to the bone of this day-in-day-out struggle, and of no chance for rest, reflection or study.

These thoughts and feelings kept emerging; but she had hardly a moment to really consider them seriously, as each new day, the Dong-il problems seemed to get more serious. Then, right in the middle of the struggle, after going to Pusan and speaking at the prayer meeting there, she was arrested and found herself sitting in a cell, asking God why. Why had Cho been taken her from the workers at such a crucial time?

Then like a flash of lightning, she knew. "Aha! That's it! I said I wanted to rest, I said I wanted to study, I said I needed time to pray. And this is my opportunity! Thank you, Lord. I'll make good use of this time you have given me."

When she was imprisoned, her physical condition was really run-down, but she found a warmth among the other prisoners. Once she was confined to bed for a week with a bad back. The other prisoners learned of her problem through the prison grapevine, and formed prayer groups and were praying for her recovery. Evidently, the rest and prayers had their effect, for she did improve. Today she is in better health than she was before her arrest.

As all prisoners do, Cho soon developed a daily routine. Each day she spent periods of time in prayer and Bible study, doing physical exercise, though she was allowed outside for exercise only 30 minutes a day, and reading. She read 150 books during her 13 months of imprisonment.

Though she had received a five-year sentence which was later commuted to three years, she was among those who were released after the assassination of Park Chung Hee in October 1979.

Upon her release, in late December, she immediately went to Inchon to see the Dong-il workers. She had hopes that their situation had improved, but she found that things were much the same. Rev. Cho had told the police during her interrogation in Pusan that she had decided to retire from U.I.M. work, but that their treatment of the Dong-il workers and her own arrest had convinced her, much to their chagrin, that she was still needed and would continue to work indefinitely. When she returned to Inchon, she found some of the women were still having to live in the U.I.M. office. She felt again the ache in her heart for these young workers who had sacrificed so much, but had so few to advocate their cause or to join in their suffering with them.

She said shortly after her release, "I haven't been able to sleep at night, worrying about them. Now I feel sure that this work is what I'll give the rest of my life to. Though the problems often seem to be insurmountable, I just have to keep on, and with God's help, I will."

NOTES

1. It is Korean custom to take off your shoes when entering a building.
2. "Plight of Women Workers, Korea," by Judy Weidman. *Response*, October 1978, p.16.

SOURCES

Interview of Cho, Wha Soon, by Walter and Louise Durst, December 31, 1979.

Cho, Wha Soon, *Inchon U.I.M. Activity Report*, January 1973-June 1975.

Ogle, George E. *Liberty to the Captives*, John Knox Press.

Weidman, Judy. "Plight of Women Workers, Korea," *Response*, October 1978, pp. 16-17.

Women's Problems Conference Report, June 29-30, 1978, Korea NCC.

Part of Korea's industrial section.

Chapter VI:
FROM HAN TO JOY—INTERPRETING THE STRUGGLES OF THE MINJUNG

In the folk song "Arirang" and in the story of Ok-nyo, the common people of Korea can be seen trudging along a troublesome road, always hoping that a brighter sun would shine upon them.

What have they learned? Was their bitter experience without meaning? What has helped them make sense of their lives? What can all Christians learn from the history of common people?

In this chapter, some folk stories are more closely examined and four interpretations are considered:

1) the **Silhak** ("Real Life") movement started by dissident Confucian scholars in the early 19th century, and its spiritual descendents;
2) the **Tonghak** ("Eastern Learning") movement which arose in the latter part of the 19th century;
3) the Protestant **churches** influenced by the early missionaries;
4) the **Minjung** (people) theologians of recent years.

INSIGHTS FROM THE PEOPLE'S CULTURE

Thanks to the language of hangul, Korea offers an abundant store of writings produced by the people themselves. Hangul was invented by scholars in the reign of Sejong, who presented it himself in 1446 as a gift of language to the common people.

The Tale of Shimchung There once was a blind man named Shim, Bongsa. He lived in a tiny fishing village with his faithful wife, who worked day and night to provide their livelihood. Weakened by hard work, she died in childbirth, leaving her helpless husband with a baby daughter. The father, reduced to begging, went from house to house asking for milk and food. Had it not been for the warm compassion ("injung") of the village women, he and the baby would not have survived.

When the daughter, Shimchung, became 10 years old, she insisted that her father stay at home. From now on she would take on the daily rounds of begging for their food.

One day while Shimchung was away, her father wandered down to the river bank. He fell in and almost drowned. Fortunately, a monk happened to pass by and pulled him out.

In the course of talking with the monk, expressing his gratitude, Shim made a serious mistake. He promised to give the temple 300 bushels of rice in return for their prayers to restore his sight.

Where could he possibly get that much rice? It became a heavy burden for the father and his loyal daughter.

One day, a group of sea merchants came to the village. They wanted to buy a young girl to offer as a sacrifice to the sea gods in return for a safe voyage. Shimchung heard the news and went in secret to the merchants. She sold herself for 300 bushels of rice.

When her father and the villagers heard what she had done, they wept and grieved over Shimchung. But there was nothing they could do. The bargain had been made. Shimchung was thrown in the ocean as an offering to the angry waves.

But the one God in heaven saw what had happened and had pity on the faithful daughter. God not only saved her from the ocean, but made her the queen of all the land. What good fortune it was for her! But Shimchung wasn't happy. Everyday as she sat in her palace, she thought about her father and wondered what had happened to him.

One day she had an idea. She would give a great feast and invite all the blind people in the country to come to the palace. Day after day, they streamed in through the giant doors and feasted on the sumptuous food. But Shimchung's father was not among them.

On the last day of the feast, she finally saw him coming into the palace. She ran to him and threw her arms around him. "Father!" she cried out in joy.

"What is this?" her father exclaimed. "Can it be true that my daughter is still alive? Oh, if I could only see her!" As soon as he said this, his eyes were opened. He saw his daughter and all the splendor of the palace around her.

The Story of Chun Hyang
In the city of Namwon in Chulla Province, there lived a retired ki-saeng, who had an exceptionally beautiful daughter named Chun Hyang, or Spring Fragrance.

On one beautiful day in May, Yi, Doryung, the mayor's son, met Chun Hyang. They fell in love at first sight and got married secretly. Yi, Doryung was afraid to tell his parents because he knew they would never accept a daughter-in-law from such a different background. He made up his mind to keep the marriage a secret until he passed the national examination and obtained a respectable position in government. Then he could arrange a marriage suitable for his station in life and also take a concubine — Chun Hyang, of course.

The trouble started when Doryung's father was promoted to a higher spot in Seoul and the family had to move up to the capital. The young lovers could hardly think of being separated, but they could bear it knowing that they would be reunited.

But the real trouble came from Pyun, Hak-do, a very evil man who became the new mayor of Namwon. He had heard of Chun Hyang's legendary beauty and wanted to have her as his concubine.

Of course, this was not acceptable to Chun Hyang, who was determined to be faithful to her secret husband even though she had not received a single letter from him since he went away. The mayor was infuriated with her rebuff and had Chun Hyang beaten and put in stocks in the prison. Half-dead from the beating, Chun Hyang cried over her fate and wondered what Doryung was doing in Seoul.

Many months went by. Up in the capital, Li, Doryung had passed the national examination with flying colors and was appointed to be a Royal Inspector for Chulla Province. With his soldiers, he entered Namwon in disguise to investigate the charges of corruption against the mayor.

But he discovered not only the mayor's wrong-doings, but also his own. The villagers, not knowing his true identity, railed against the heartless, faithless Li, Doryung for his neglect of the faithful Chun Hyang.

In the happy ending, Li, Doryung repents of his neglect, punishes the wicked mayor and takes Chun Hyang to Seoul as his wife. But the villagers had learned that you'd better not count on the upper class.

The Tale of Hong, Kil-Dong
This is the story of Hong, Kil-Dong, the son of a concubine. He was bright and talented and in spite of his low status, had obtained some learning. But he didn't have a chance in the world. Finally, rebelling against the whole system, he left home and joined a group of bandits in the mountains.

His natural abilities caused him to rise and he quickly became the head of the group. He reorganized them into a "Party for Revitalization of the Poor."

They raided evil governors and majors, robbed wicked rich people and distributed their wealth among the poor people.

Naturally, the government leaders tried to stop the movement, but they couldn't. Hong, Kil-Dong was too strong and clever for them. Why, he even had a secret power by which he could control the rain.

Finally, the king made Hong, Kil-Dong's father go to his son and ask him to stop the movement. Kil-Dong as a loyal son, could not disobey his father's request. Taking his followers in a boat, he sailed to an island called Yul-to and created a perfect country with justice and equality as the founding principles.

MAIN POINTS IN THE STORIES

The simplicity of the stories masks their cleverness. In each, a traditional virtue is first praised. But then the tables are turned and the people express their deeper feelings.

1. In Shimchung's story, the traditional virtue which is praised is "hyo," the filial loyalty of a

child to its parents, and one of the main tenets of Confucian teaching. But this was not why the people loved the story so much.

What they loved was the feeling of compassion ("injung") which permeated the whole story. It moved from heart to heart, from event to event, from the time when the women — even the wealthy ones — cared for Shimchung and her widowed father to the time when the whole village and even the sea merchants wept over her miserable fate. Even God was moved by the compassion of the people to save Shimchung.

Why did this quality have such power to move people? It isn't hard to see. Living in a cruel world, the people yearned for compassion. They wanted all human relationships to be compassionate. They even wanted the rich women and the money-grubbing merchants to let compassion rule their hearts. At least in their imaginations, it could come true.

2. What were the people trying to say as they sang and recited Chun Hyang's story? The traditional virtue they praised was faithfulness, this time that of the wife to her husband, another major Confucian teaching.

But the deeper feeling being expressed was anger. The story contrasts the behavior of the upper classes with that of the common people. The former are brutal and heartless while the latter are warm and full of compassion. The former are inhumane while the latter are human through and through. The story allowed the people to express their real feelings toward faithless and untrustworthy rulers.

Listen to what one of the villagers told Yi Doryung while he was still in disguise:

"That young beggar Li, who went off and left her, has never sent a word of news to her. I don't care what rank he has risen to. He isn't worth the water in my chamber pot."

As they sang and recited, the people could feel good because they knew they were more noble than the gentry who despised them. As they waited for a new leader, where could they look? To the upper classes? No, they couldn't be respected or counted on. They would look for their new leaders among themselves.

3. Hong, Kil-Dong's story is the story of the Minjung's messiah. This story must have been very healing, as they told one another how Kil-Dong raided the rich to give to the poor. They laughed as the wicked rulers became so afraid of Kil-Dong and begged him to leave. Even the king had to recognize Kil-Dong's superior strength and power.

But the greatest satisfaction must have been the dream of a future to come when all social distinctions and barriers would be destroyed and justice would be the rule. Anyone who would say that the Korean people are not ready for freedom simply does not understand their centuries-old longing for equality and justice. And all of this would come from the people themselves. The story of Hong, Kil-Dong helped greatly to lift the consciousness and self-esteem of the people.

These stories were often told with masks, another aspect of the people's culture. Hiding their true identities behind the masks, they could take on new identities, jabbing at the weaknesses of the upper class, "unmasking" their false strength with puns and jokes. Through the folk dramas, the people's self-confidence grew. Step by step, they prepared themselves to take the future into their own hands.

THE PEOPLE'S CULTURE AND SOCIAL REFORM

Silhak One of the reform movements growing out of the exprience of the common life was the Silhak Movement of the early 17th century. This period was a particularly difficult one. Power in the countryside was monopolized by a few corrupt families who gained control of most of the farmland. Things were so bad that many yangban or upper class people were reduced to working for their livelihood. Countless farmers became landless.

In the cities, wealth similarly shifted into the hands of only a few powerful merchants. Many small businesses went bankrupt. The whole society was in a shambles. And the ruling class at the palace spent their time in hot dispute over minute aspects of Confucian doctrine irrelevant to the burning issues of the day.

Confronted with this sad situation, a group of scholars started the movement called Silhak, the Study of Real Life. (See Chapter III.) Most of the scholars who joined the movement were those who had been demoted from the power center and had become acquainted first-hand with the ugly reality of ordinary life.

They advocated a new kind of learning for the purpose of effective government and the proper use of power. Although their studies centered around politics, economics and social studies, they also covered administration, agriculture, commerce and technology.

The most outstanding scholar of the movement was Chung Yak Young, who from 1801 spent eighteen years in exile. He produced a considerable body of written work which aimed at improving the ordinary life of people.

The influence of the Silhak Movement on succeeding generations of Koreans was immense. Most importantly, it broke the hold that Confucianism had on scholarship. Since then, countless intellectuals have believed that the task of the educated person is to stand beside the oppressed and work with them.

Tonghak Tonghak, or the Eastern Learning Movement, was the spiritual heir of the Silhak Movement. It sprang out of the soil of han (suffering) about the end of the 19th century.

Choi, Je-Oo, the founder of the movement, was born in 1824, like the mythical Hong, Kil-Dong, the son of a concubine. Although he was brilliant and well-educated, he couldn't get a position in society because of who his mother was. At the age of 31, he left home and became a wanderer among the people.

Choi wandered for five years, witnessing and experiencing every kind of misery. He returned home in 1860, and fell ill, burdened with the memories of all he had seen.

Delirious with fever, he had a vision of God who entrusted him with a new mission and a new teaching. The heart of the new teaching was "in nae ch'on," which translates literally to mean "the human person is heaven." God was in the cries of the han-ridden people. The divine will was in the yearning for compassion (injung) and social justice. By serving people, one served God.

Choi preached the goal of an egalitarian society. He advocated the elimination of all inequalities in the social system. At the same time he warned against greed, which he saw as the source of all evil. He encouraged people not to lose heart, that a new age was about to dawn.

This teaching caught people's imagination and spread among them like wildfire. The government, which was very unstable at the time, was threatened. Choi, Je-Oo was arrested and executed as a "heretic."

The death of the founder, however, could not stop the movement. On the contrary, it spread more rapidly among the people after his death and finally erupted into a revolutionary war in 1894 under the leadership of Chun, Pong-joon, another alienated scholar. The war progressed favorably for the Tonghak Farmer's Revolutionary Army.

They presented thoroughly humanitarian demands (see Chapter I) filled with injung. Note especially points five and six. They were especially mindful of the humiliating flat hat worn by butchers, the lowest class of people. They were also paying special attention to young widows who were not permitted to remarry because of strict Confucian traditions.

Had it not been for the intervention of the Japanese Imperial Army at this time and their support of the shaky Yi government, history might have been different.

Although the Tonghak lost the war on the battleground, the spirit of the movement was never lost. It has come back time and time again and revitalized the Minjung's movement. In particular, the March First Independence Movement in 1919 was started by Tonghak leaders such as Sohn, Pyung-hee. Even now, a great many intellectuals and human rights leaders in Korea proudly claim to be the heirs of the Tonghak spirit.

The Protestant Church The Protestant Church has also played a major role in reform of injustices. As we saw in Chapter One, Koreans welcomed the missionaries from America. They wanted to learn all they could about this religion which came from a strong and free nation. To them the Good News of Jesus Christ was also the good news for a free and just Korea.

Excerpts from the Korea Church Press of 1896 and 1898 reflect this sentiment:

"We hope sincerely that the church will prosper around Seoul. Thereby the nation will be modernized."

"I am hoping that through the steady growth of the church, the nation will eventually be modernized."

The early missionaries were highly trained, intelligent and articulate people, excellent representatives not only of the church but of modern, scientific learning. Thus the church grew by leaps and bounds.

The picture changed as the aggressiveness of the Japanese occupational government became more overt. Differences of opinion regarding national independence developed between the missionaries and the Koreans.

Seeing that the church was becoming a target of Japanese oppression, most of the missionaries began to advocate separation of politics and religion. They doubtless had only the safety of the people in mind, but unfortunately their concern also had negative results. Some of the missionaries went so far as to speak out against Korean patriotic actions, and leveled particularly negative criticism at the Tonghak movement. A few even agreed with the Japanese and publicly praised Governor-General Ito's policies.

This is what M. C. Harris wrote in 1907 to the "Yomiuri Daily," a newspaper in Japan:

"We, well-known missionaries (Johnson, Scranton and Harris) have been threatened with death for having refused to help the resistance movement against the protective measures of the Agreement. . . . I personally think that the policy of Governor Ito is praiseworthy. I confess that I am one of its most ardent supporters."

Although such remarks came from an inadequate understanding of Korean feelings and an ill-placed trust in Japanese intentions, the Korean people were greatly disappointed. Deeply hurt, many called for the missionaries to go home.

The tension mounted. The missionaries were going through torment, seeing their beloved friends rebelling against them. The Koreans felt guilt in spite of their anger — hadn't the missionaries come far away from home to a remote land to deliver the Good News of Jesus Christ? Weren't many of their babies and coworkers buried in Korean soil?

The great revival movement which erupted in 1907 was a resolution of sorts of the deep torment of Korean Christians and missionaries alike. Koreans buried their lost identity in the church and devoted themselves fully to its development, but they never stopped thinking about freedom.

Later when the wrongness of the Japanese policy was fully apparent, it was easier for foreigners to accept the role Christians would play. This note was recorded by the U.S. Council of Churches at the time: "It is an identical thing in Korea today to be a Christian and to participate in the demonstration for national independence."

A second mission policy which produced both positive and negative results concerned the theological education of Korean pastors. The missionaries deliberately put a limit on the higher education of Korean clergy.

To understand the good intentions of this policy, remember that the earliest preaching of the gospel had been directed toward the masses of people in the lower classes. This policy deserves praise. Not only was it true to the way Jesus preached, it was forward-looking as well, for a modern nation requires an enlightened citizenry.

The aim of the policy to give Korean ministers education only slightly higher than that of the common people was so rapport could be maintained. To a great degree, the policy worked.

The negative results are apparent. As it grew, the Korean church could not speak for itself theologically. It remained dependent on missionary sources of education and an imported theology which was inadequate because it was not related to the people's everyday experience.

Things were not to remain that way. A new breed of theologian began to emerge in the 1930s. They began to insist that Korean ministers should enjoy the freedom of theological inquiry and become acquainted with the whole range of theological thought.

This group of young ministers encountered much opposition and had to endure scathing criticism. The result was that they were excluded from the mainstream, but they continued to work in their isolation. They survived the bitter days of the early forties, to surface again after emancipation from Japan in 1945.

The chief advocate of this movement was Dr. Kim, Chai Choon. He had many followers and finally succeeded in creating a climate wherein Korean theologians could freely air their views and convictions. Although Dr. Kim himself did not produce an indigenous systematic theology, he set progressive thinking into motion which would result in an indigenous theology.

Minjung Many stormy and stress-filled years passed before this new indigenous theology emerged, based on the long history of the people's suffering. The bitter war between northern and southern Korea, the Rhee regime, the 1961 Student Revolution, the military coup of 1962 and the subsequent strong-man rule of General Park, Chung Hee — all of these played a part in the slow evolution of another people's resistance movement. In its latter days, the Park government was able to rule only by a succession of emergency decrees. Under the decrees, hundreds of professors were forced out of the schools and universities. The prisons were filled with young students, women and men. Labor leaders, lawyers, reporters, ministers and priests followed them.

Among those imprisoned were a number of theologians and one of the writers of this book. We, too, had been expelled from teaching posts for having joined in the justice movement. Because we had lost our jobs, we were able to join in the minjung's struggle full-time and learned of minjung's agonies and aspirations from firsthand experience.

The prison experiences became a wonderful blessing. The lonely cells became the best theological classes ever attended. As Christians sat in lonely cells, often in solitary confinement, they listened to the cries of the han-ridden criminals. Perspectives on life were completely transformed. Why did there have to be such han (suffering)? What had the church been doing? Had the church been listening to these people at all? Did the church really understand the minjung to whom it were supposed to be preaching the gospel of Jesus Christ? What does the God of the Bible have to do with these criminals? Common people? What does the Bible say about all these contradictions?

These were really agonizing questions and imprisoned Christians knew that they themselves could not escape from blame. As the Bible was read with these burning questions, it became a new book. Christians discovered a similar minjung in the Bible.

What understanding of God was gained from reading the Bible under the bright light of the people's story?

1. *Han is the starting point of God's salvation history.* Kim, Chi Ha, noted poet and Catholic layman, defined the concept of han this way (in a free translation from his "Prison Memorandum"):

"Han is the minjung's angry and sad sentiment turned inward, hardened and stuck to their hearts. The anger and sadness are stuck so much that it could stay forever in their hearts, discharging resentment, anguish, yearning and a desire for revenge."

Han is created when people's fundamental humanity is not recognized. When they are not respected. When the image of God in each person is not recognized. As the blood of Abel cried out from the ground, han demands revenge so that justice may be done.

Han is the starting point for a new history because God hears the cry. In han, people meet the loving, compassionate God who justifies the cry of the minjung and promises them a new land. Moses met Yahweh in the burning bush, Jesus emerged from despised Nazareth. Choi Je-Oo heard God's voice after years of wandering among the outcasts. Anyone who wants to meet this God and make a new beginning, must "go to Galilee" where the oppressed and poor are gathered.

2. *Greed is the cause of the vicious circle of evil.*

"What good is it to have slaves liberated?," people often ask. "Liberated slaves become worse tyrants." It seems to be true. Human history is often witness to such a vicious circle of evil. Korean people had longed eagerly for freedom and democracy. Yet, what happened to them after the national emancipation? Are they not still suffering just the same under their own rulers? It was the same with the Israelites. After they were delivered from Egypt, the kings and rulers of Israel oppressed their own people.

According to Choi, Je-Oo, greed caused the vicious circle. It was easy for him to see this, because he knew that the rulers of the time should govern the people with "In," the spirit of charity, as Confucianism demanded. Yet he saw all around him that things were happening in the opposite way. It was clear to him that the source of the trouble was greed.

The prophets of the Bible, including John the Baptist and Jesus of Nazareth, said the same thing. Listen to Micah.

"Shame on those who lie in bed planning evil and wicked deeds, and rise at daybreak to do them, knowing that they have the power.

They covet land and take it by force;
    if they want a house, they seize it;
they rob a man of his home
    and steal everyman's inheritance." (2:1-3)

Here is what Jesus said.

"Alas for you, lawyers and Pharisees. You clean the outside of cup and dish, which you have filled inside by robbery and self-indulgenece. Blind Pharisee. Clean the inside of the cup first; then the outside will be clean also." (Mt. 23:25-26)

But one wonders why people so readily fall into the trap. The historians of Solomon's time pondered upon the issue very seriously as they lamented over their king who had fallen into the trap, too. The report in the beginning chapters of the Book of Genesis describes how the life became blessed and complete as a man and a woman were united in injung (See Chapter Two). Then the couple fell into the trap. Pay attention to what Eve said to herself as she looked at the forbidden fruit. (It could as easily have been Adam.) She said, "It is good to eat, pleasing to the eye, and tempting to contemplate." (3:6a) It was the attraction of material things which blinded her and she was not able to see the spiritual aspect of life. Once this happened, there was ruthless competition (4:1-16) followed by the arrogance of the mighty (4:19-26). What happens to those who do not have the power? They become like trash only to be swept away (Chs. 6-8).

On the other hand, the mighty ones become so confident that they plot to overthrow the heavenly king. (Ch. 11).

The same analysis is found in the Tale of Chun Hyang. Pyun, Hak-do, the new governor in the story, was not really that bad at the outset. He was simply fun loving and somewhat irresponsible, but no more. When the saw Chun Hyang, his appetite was whipped up. To him, she was a forbidden fruit, good to eat and pleasing to the eye, and tempting to contemplate. She was simply a thing to be possessed and sight of her spiritual side was lost. Yes, the root of the trouble is people's inability to see others as whole beings because their view is obstructed by physical and material attraction.

3. *Dan, "Cutting", is a necessary act of salvation.*

Liberation from external oppression is necessary for anyone to be truly human. But to be free from greed is equally necessary. For this Kim, Chi Ha advocated dan in his prison memo. One has to cut one's self off from greed. The prophets of the Old Testament preached the same theme to their contemporaries. The repentance which John the Baptist and Jesus called for meant the same thing.

But how is dan possible? Kim, Chi Ha himself experienced the difficulty of it. He expressed it in this prayer in his prison cell:

"O, God. I have been offering the same prayer for months. Listen to my prayer, O, Lord. Sharpen the sword in me. Grant me the courage to take the act of dan, even if my heart bursts in pain, so that I can start the journey for the battlefield...Ah. Help me to cut off for the far away journey. I cannot cut off the tie that draws me into the flowery tomb of happy pleasurable home, the nest of amnesia. Help me to cut the little leafy hands and the blinking eyes of the meek woman. Help me cut, cut, cut off from that tie.

Send me off to the wilderness, dawning under the cold wintry stars, where I can gain the maddeningly bitter awakening!"

Kim, Chi Ha discovered further that dan is an act much more difficult for those whose human rights have been deprived for centuries. Again in his prison memo, he says,

"Starvation . . . the earth is full of starvation . . . Age-old starvation . . . limitless appetite . . . limitless greed . . . the birth of devils!"

Perhaps the greed which possessed the Israelites was caused by their age-old starvation also.

So far we have been discussing the greed caused by a normal appetite, but how about greed coupled with the desire for revenge? Most deprived people have this inclination. They say, "You have had it long enough. Let me have it now. I have a right to live exactly as you have been living." This comes from an innate sense of justice, and it is not easy to dissuade people from taking such action. To free one's self from such an obsession is to free one's self from the curse of han. It requires a miraculous change of heart and only the Holy Spirit can do it. Thus we wait for the Messiah to come.

4. *The Bottom is the Womb for the Messiah.*

According to biblical tradition, the Messiah was to be conceived and grow in a womb which had never been used by another baby. Kim, Chi Ha presents the bottom of society as such a womb. Has anyone ever heard that a Messiah could be born from the bottom? Ask Nathaniel. He could not believe that anything good could come from Nazareth. (John 1:46)

What did Chi Ha mean about the Messiah coming from the bottom? Chang, Il-dam, his fictional version of the Messiah, was a descendant of three generations of butchers and three generations of prostitutes. Chang, Il-dam really came from the lowest womb possible.

Why does he have to come from the bottom? There seems to be a two-fold answer to the question. First, he had to experience han and hate evil so thoroughly that he would never be able to compromise with it. Secondly, the desire for revenge had to be transformed into a positive freedom. Kim, Chi Ha's story has it this way:

One day, Chang, Il-dam encountered a dying prostitute giving birth to a child. She was surrounded by her prostitute friends. At the sight, he cried out,

"Ah, from a rotten body comes a new life. It is God who is coming." He knelt down and said, "God is in your womb. God is in the bottom. Oh, my mother," and he kissed her feet.

Chang, Il-dam found a caring community around the dying prostitute. He encountered God being born there. He knelt down and kissed her feet, saying, "Oh, my mother."

With this experience, the fictional Chang, Il-dam was able to take the act of dan in a positive way. He discovered that treasure in the fellowship of the community. Selling everything, he purchased the treasure. He was ready to take up the role of the Messiah.

It was the same way with Jesus. He was born and raised in Galilee, a place which was rejected and despised. From early childhood he saw and experienced terrible human miseries caused by all kinds of evil. He was often tempted to join the revolutionary movement which was prevalent around him. But he was always suspicious of an act coming out of hatred. Then he encountered warm communities filled with the spirit of injung, love in the midst of people who were called sinners. In these communities he experienced the living God. The life in those communities meant so much to him that he decided to give up everything for it. At the age of 30, he left everything behind him and set out to preach the "koinonia" which he called the New Age of God. He was taking up the role of the Messiah.

5. *Exorcism (Cleansing) is the Role of the Messiah.*

The work of the Messiah is to bring about the cosmic koinonia in which there will be no more crying, no more tears. In order to achieve this goal, however, the Messiah must take on the role of exorcist, casting out the spirit of greed and enmity from individual hearts as well as from the social system.

Look at what Chang, Il-dam did after he achieved his own dan. Kim, Chi Ha did not elaborate what kind of community it was nor how he taught about dan. It can be safely assumed that it was a community bound by the spirit of injung in which the members could have that renewing and revitalizing experience. Then he must have explained meaning and significance in this new experience in comparison to their old han producing experiences, urging them to cut themselves off from greed and the desire to take revenge. Through this warm experience and enlightenment, they would be cleansed gradually and become new persons. This is precisely what Jesus did with his disciples.

Chang, Il-dam gathered his disciples around him and marched to Seoul, the heartland of all evil, with empty cups in their hands, singing the refrain "Rice is heaven."

"Rice is heaven.
As you cannot go to heaven alone,
so rice is to be shared.
Rice is heaven.
As you watch the stars in heaven together,
so rice is to be shared with man.
Rice is heaven.
As you take rice into your mouth,
you receive heaven in your body.
Rice is heaven.
Ah, rice is
for everyone to share."

They, as a community, are now challenging the evil system in order to expel the evil from it. The empty cans in their hands symbolize how they are now free from greed. The song they sing is the incantation by which evil is to be exorcised from the society. In the phrase "rice is heaven," the spirit and matter have become one.

The same message is beautifully taught in the 25th chapter of the Gospel according to Matthew where the last judgment is described. Jesus Christ says that whatever is done as a concrete act of injung (compassion) to one of the society's lowest, is done to God.

Concluding Remarks Christians are asked to follow such a Messiah. The demand seems very stiff and the road appears very rugged. How are Christians going to be able to follow it?

Here is a story which might answer the question.

There is a small Christian community in Seoul which is called the Galilee Church. It has an attendance of only 30 on the average. They meet every Sunday afternoon, in the sanctuary of another church which is courageous enough to let them in. For the community is composed of ex-professors and reporters, former prisoners of conscience and families of political prisoners. Most people wouldn't expect much from such a small congregation.

Yet, as one enters the church the spirit which is unique to this church is evident. The whole service is permeated with a tremendous sense of joy; yet, there is a true sharing of pain. It is informal throughout the service; yet there is a due seriousness. It is a very close knit community; yet it is open to newcomers and visitors, even the KCIA agents assigned to observe. It is an alive community with a clear sense of direction.

They all have tough stories to tell, but they are joyous and lively. If asked how they bear all the troubles they confront on the way, they will say to you:

"We have not chosen this. No one really did. We were all somehow pushed into this by God. As we walk along with other friends, however, we experience the spirit of injung embracing us, enlightening us, and strengthening us. As we work together and pray together, we experience God living in our midst and we experience joy swelling within us. So we keep marching along believing that it is Christ who leads us, granting joy on the way."

The han-ridden journey over Arirang Mountain has been transformed into a joy-filled march with the Anointed One in the very midst of it.

QUESTIONS

1. Why were the songs and stories written by the common people written in "hangul" instead of Chinese characters?

2. Can you think of songs and stories from this country which have served the same purpose as the ones mentioned in this chapter? Make a list of them and look at the words.

3. How did you feel as you read the story of Korean and missionary relationships during the Japanese occupation of Korea? Is there a parallel in this country's history?

4. How do you do Bible study? How is it similar or different to the way described in this Chapter?

5. What new ideas came to you about God, about Jesus and the Church as you read this chapter?

A group of entertainers performing the "Farmer's Dance" celebrating spring planting.

A FOLK STORY AND A FOLK SONG

A Folk Story: "THE TALE OF OKNYO"

(Editor's Note: This story is usually called "The Tale of Pyung Kangso," who was one of Oknyo's husbands in the ancient story. But since it was the woman who survived and did all the suffering, we have called it "her story"! The tenacity of the minjung is its theme.)

Once upon a time in a remote mountain village lived a young girl named Oknyo. She was very beautiful. When she was 15 years old, her parents gave her in marriage to the son of another village family. But tragedy struck and the new husband died suddenly on their wedding night.

Other marriages were arranged. But each ended in the same way. By the time she was 19, Oknyo had been married five times!

The villagers were frightened, then angry. They said that it was all Oknyo's fault. So they put her out of the village and she was doomed to wander through the mountains without family or friends for the rest of her life.

One day she while was walking along, she met a robust and carefree young man, Pyung Kangso, who was singing and dancing on the path. He fell in love with Oknyo immediately and asked her to marry him. So she did.

But life was not easy. Pyung Kangso's fun-loving ways did not match married life. But Oknyo was grateful to him and worked hard to support them both. He was her hope against a life of wandering.

One day she begged him to help her get some wood for the cooking fire. Although he didn't like to work, this time he agreed and went off to the forest.

On his way, he spotted two wooden totem poles standing by the roadside. This would save him a long trip, he thought! So he carried them home and started to chop them up.

Oknyo ran out of the house in a panic. Totem poles were houses for the spirits and they would be angry if their houses were destroyed. But Kangso laughed at his wife's foolishness and went on with his chopping.

Sure enough, a few days later he was struck down with a fatal illness. Oknyo's fragile hope was shattered.

As the sad news spread, young men from the surrounding villages flocked in, each offering his help to bury the deceased. For Oknyo was very beautiful, and each one hoped to marry her.

But as each man reached to lift the body, they fell dead on the spot! Now instead of one dead man to bury, Oknyo was surrounded by them. Her fate turned from bad to worse.

At just that moment, Deop-duggi, another gad-about much like Park Kangso, appeared on the scene. He took one look at Oknyo and asked her to marry him on the spot. He sent for a Shaman and with her help, the spirits were calmed down and all the dead men were buried.

Oknyo could not believe her good fortune. Preparations were made for the wedding. But at the last minute, the fickle Deop-duggi changed his mind and went back home, leaving the hapless Oknyo alone.

The story ends with Oknyo starting out again on her lonely journey over Arirang Mountain. She is in tears. But then the crying stops and her step quickens. Who knows? She might meet another young man just around the bend and live happily ever after!

A Folk Song: "ARIRANG"

Ask any Korean to name a typical folk song, and nine times out of ten, it will be "Arirang." It is the best example of the melancholy feeling permeating Korean folk music.

"Arirang" is the name of a mountain pass. In Korean custom the chorus is sung by the group and each member in turn sings a solo on the verses. People pride themselves on the number of verses they know to this song, especially if the verse is unknown to the others. It is common, too, for inspiration to strike (melancholy, humor or both) and new verses will be created on the spot.

ARIRANG

Korean Folk Song

A ri rang___ A ri rang___ A ra ri___ yo___

A ri rang___ Cross - ing___ ov - er the___ hill,

car - ry - ing a child on her back. Cross - ing___ the___ hill,___

how great a__ wo - man's__ sac - ri - fice.___

Arirang

NEVER FORGET

Never forget
the bare mountain last spring reviving
with waves of red azaleas
bursting up from streaks of snow;
and beyond the resurrecting mountain,
the skies.

Never forget
the roaring waterfall;
and rising forth amidst the waterfall
the strong young bamboo.

After being led away in chains
after the long, long ordeal is ended,
long after all others have forgotten,
suddenly standing again by my side
the presence of friends.

by Kim Chi Ha

THEOLOGICAL DECLARATION OF KOREAN CHRISTIANS, 1973

Issued on May 20, 1973, despite government restrictions on all criticism, this underground declaration by a group of Christian ministers in Korea grounds the struggle for democracy in the Christian faith, charts the course of that struggle, and calls for solidarity of the churches throughout the world; it also serves to introduce the meaning of the Korean democratic struggle to the world community.

We make this declaration in the name of the Korean Christian community. But under the present circumstances, in which one man controls all the powers of the three branches of government and uses military arms and the intelligence network to oppress the people, we hesitate to reveal those who signed this document. We must fight and struggle in the underground until our victory is achieved.

The historical situation of the Korean people has been very grave since last October. President Park's consolidation of power has had certain demonic consequences for the life of the Korean nation and people.

The Christian community, as an integral part of the Korean people, now stands up and speaks out on the present situation, compelled by the divine mandates of the Messianic Kingdom.

Since World War II, our people have gone through trials and sufferings, of social chaos, economic deprivation, and especially the tragic Korean War and the resulting political dictatorships. It has been an ardent aspiration of our people that a new and humane community might be restored to their lives. However, the hopes of the people for such a restoration of humane community has been cruelly crushed by President Park in his absolutization of dictatorship and ruthless political repression. This is done in the name of the so-called October Revitalization, a set of false promises which is only the sinister plan of some evil men.

We, the Christians in Korea, are compelled to speak out and take accompanying actions on the following grounds:

(1)   We are under God's command that we should be faithful to His Word in concrete historical situations. It is not a sense of triumphant victory that moves us today; rather it is a sense of confession of our sins before God; and yet we are commanded by God to speak the truth and act in the present situation in Korea.

(2)   The people in Korea are looking up to Christians and urging us to take action in the present grim situation. It is not because we deserve to represent them. We have often fallen short of their deeper expectations, and yet we are urged and encouraged to move on this course of action, not because we envision ourselves as the representatives of our people, but because we are moved by their agony to call upon God for their deliverance from evil days.

(3)   We stand in a historical tradition of such struggles for liberation as the independence movement by Christians against Japanese colonialism. We realize that our Christian community has often lacked the courage to take a decisive stand, and that the theological outlook of the official bodies of our Christian churches has been too pietistic to take up revolutionary roles. However, we do not feel disheartened by the weakness of some of our brothers; rather we are determined to seek our theological convictions from the historical traditions of our churches.

The firm foundation of our words and deeds is our faith in God the Lord of history, in Jesus the proclaimer of the Messianic Kingdom, and in the Spirit who moves vigorously among the people. We believe that God is the ultimate vindicator of the oppressed, the weak, and the poor; He judges the evil forces in history. We believe that Jesus the Messiah proclaimed the coming of the Messianic Kingdom, to be subversive to the evil powers, and that his messianic Kingdom will be the haven of the dispossessed, the rejected, and the downtrodden. We also believe that the Spirit is working for the new creation of history and cosmos, as well as for the regeneration and sanctification of individual man.

In this grave historical situation, we as a Christian community believe

(1)   that we are commanded by God to be representatives before God the Judge and Lord of History, to pray that the suffering and oppressed people may be set free.

(2)   that we are commanded by our Lord Jesus Christ to live among the oppressed, the poor, and the despised as he did in Judea; and that we are summoned to stand up and speak the truth to the powers that be, as he did before Pontius Pilate of the Roman Empire.

(3) that we are compelled by the Spirit to participate in his transforming power and movement for the creation of a new society and history, as well as for the transformation of our character; and that this Spirit is the Spirit of Messianic Kingdom who commands us to struggle for sociopolitical transformation in this world.

Therefore, we express our theological convictions on the following issues:

(1) The present dictatorship in Korea is destroying rule by law and persuasion; it now rules by force and threat alone. Community is being turned into jungle. In fact no one is above the law except God; worldly power is entrusted by God to civil authority to keep justice and order in human society. If anyone poses himself above the law and betrays the divine mandate for justice, he is in rebellion against God. Oriental tradition, too, understands that good rule is carried out through the moral persuasion and virtue of the ruler. One may conquer people by the sword; but they cannot be ruled by the sword.

(2) The regime in Korea is destroying freedom of conscience and freedom of religious belief. There is freedom neither of expression nor of silence. There is interference by the regime in Christian churches' worship, prayer gatherings, content of sermons, and teaching of the Bible.

The Christian Church and other religious bodies must be the defenders of conscience for the people; for destruction of conscience is a most demonic act. In defending the freedom of religious belief against interference by the regime in Korea, Christian churches are also defending freedom of conscience for the Korean people.

(3) The dictatorship in Korea is using systematic deception, manipulation, and indoctrination to control the people. The mass media has been turned into the regime's propaganda machine to tell the people half-truths and outright lies, and to control and manipulate information to deceive people.

We believe that christians are witnesses to truth, always struggling to break any system of deception and manipulation, for to tell the truth is the ultimate power that sets men free for God's Messianic Kingdom.

(4) The dictatorship in Korea uses sinister and inhuman and at the same time ruthlessly efficient means to destroy political opponents, intellectual critics, and innocent people. The use of the Korean Central Intelligence Agency (KCIA) for this

purpose is somewhat similar to the evil ways of the Nazi Gestapo or the KGB of the Stalin era. People are physically and mentally tortured, intimidated and threatened, and sometimes even disappear completely. Such treatments are indeed diabolical acts against humanity.

We believe that god has created humans in body and soul. Body as well as soul will be resurrected at the day of judgement of the Messianic Kingdom. We believe especially in the sanctity of the human body; therefore any violation of it is equal to killing a man. It is a murderous act.

(5) The present dictatorship is responsible for the economic system in Korea, in which the powerful dominate the poor. The people, poor urban workers and rural peasants, are victims of severe exploitation and social and economic injustice. So-called "economic development" in Korea turned out to be the conspiracy of a few rulers against the poor people, and a curse to our environment.

We as Christians must struggle to destroy this system of extreme dehumanization and injustice; for we are witnesses to the ongoing movement of the Messianic Kingdom in history, in which the poor will be enriched, the oppressed will be vindicated, and peach will be enjoyed by the people.

(6) The present regimes in the South and North are using the unification talks only to preserve their own power; and they are betraying the true aspirations of the people for the unification of their land. We believe as Christians that the people deeply yearn for authentic community on the basis of true reconciliation. Without transcendence beyond the past experiences of better conflict and differences in ideological and politico-economic systems, and without transformation of our historical conditions of oppression, true unification cannot be realized.

A Call For Action And Support

(1) *To the people in Korea:* Withdraw any form of recognition of the laws, orders, policies, and other political processes of dictatorship that have been wrought since October 17, 1972. Build various forms of solidarity among the people to struggle for the restoration of democracy in South Korea.

(2) *To the Christians in Korea:* As preparation for the above struggle, we Christians should renew our churches by deepening our theological thinking, by our clear stance and solidarity with the oppressed and poor, by the relevant proclamation of the gospel of the Messianic Kingdom, and by

praying for our nation; and we should prepare ourselves for martyrdom, if necessary, as our forefathers did.

(3) *To the Christians of the world*: Most of all we need your prayers and solidarity, and we ask you to express our common bond through actions of encouragement and support.

Conclusion

Jesus the Messiah, our Lord, lived and dwelt among the oppressed, poverty-stricken, and sick in Judea. He boldly stood in confrontation with Pontius Pilate, a representative of the Roman Empire, and he was crucified in the course of his witness to the truth. He has risen from the dead to release the power of transformation which sets the people free.

We resolve that we will follow the footsteps of our Lord, living among our oppressed and poor people, standing against political oppression, and participating in the transformation of history, for this is the only way to the Messianic Kingdom.

A MOTHER'S PRAYER

At the September 22, 1974 joint Catholic-Protestant prayer meeting, Mrs. Kim Myong-chin, president of the women's society of Saemunan Church and mother of two sons arrested on April 3, offered this prayer to God which moved hundreds of those present to tears.

O God, we give thanks that you loved us so much that you gave your Son that through him we might become your children, and that we have the privilege to come before you in prayer. Many mothers whose sons are imprisoned, and many others join our hearts and spirits together as mothers to pray, and so we pray that our prayer, like that of Solomon of old, may be acceptable to you, so that you may pour out upon us your blessing, beyond even that for which we pray. O, Father God, since our beloved sons have been in prison, spring has passed, and summer has changed into chilly fall, and in a few days we will be celebrating Ch'usok (Harvest Moon Festival). We cannot keep back our tears. Since there is no way to still the sorrow of our hearts, at times we have wandered around on a lonely mountaintop crying aloud to you. And we have spent night-long prayer vigils putting our plea before you with tears. Now, O God, delay no longer, but take pity on us and answer our prayer. O, God, examine our sons' hearts. They did not put their pleasures or happiness first, but truly loved their neighbors. Among them are those who served the children of Yonhidong slums, providing a night school for them. Some of them taught your word to isolated shoe-shine boys and paper boys, and comforted them. They gladly gave themselves to be friends to unfortunate orphans. They followed God's word; they were honest and despised injustice; they knew how to distinguish true from false, and helped many to realize God's love. They truly made an effort to live love. Even now, in prison, our sons are witnessing to God's word before their unbelieving brothers. We cannot but give thanks to God when we hear of their having shared even a piece of bread with others. O, God, have mercy on them; if they have done wrong, you, God, who forgive even seventy times seven, we earnestly pray that you will hasten the day when they will repent and pray for forgiveness.

Have mercy on the mother of Hwang In Sung. Comfort her in her despair which has led her to the point of trying to take her own life because her house is looked on as being that of a communist. Have pity on the mother of Kim Kyung Nam; help her as she labors by the day to keep alive and to support and help her son. Kim Young Jun's mother died without seeing her son, and her son fasted and wept for five days. Comfort his family. Besides these, many mothers are suffering greatly. We pray for all of these. We mothers often spend a night without closing our eyes. When the wind blows and it rains, we can't sleep for thinking of our sons. When we meet their friends on the street, our throats choke so that we can't speak. How can we help thinking of our sons every time we sit down to a meal? O, Jesus, how can we express all the pain in our breasts?

O, Father God, we sincerely repent before you. Have pity on this land and this people, Forgive us that in the past we were only concerned that our own children were well fed and clothed. We could not really understand the suffering of Christ's Cross; forgive us the sin of being concerned only that our own children have success in life. Forgive us, that although we saw the plight of many poverty-stricken neighbors, we did not put forth the effort to be true neighbors to them. Forgive the many mothers who have lived in luxury, loving this and ignoring the needy widows and orphans around us. Through our sons we have come to realize what you require of us mothers. It is that we should love others' children as our own. O, God, grant us faith so that we may overcome this terrible suffering we have come to serve our neighbors. Through our suffering we have come to realize just how great is Your grace. Help all of us who believe in God to work together to bring about your Kingdom on earth. We pray in the name of Jesus Christ. Amen.

FACTS AND FIGURES ON THE
NATIONAL COUNCIL OF CHURCHES IN KOREA

SIGNIFICANT DATES

September 23, 1923	Organizing meeting of the Korean National Christian Council, including churches and Christian organizations such as YWCA and YMCA
1938 - 1947	Activity ceased due to Japanese occupation and oppression of the churches
1948	Work of the Christian Council re-established
1970	Organization of the National Council of Churches in Korea (now churches only)

MEMBER CHURCHES

1. Presbyterian Church of Korea (Jesus Presbyterian)
2. The Methodist Church
3. Presbyterian Church of the Republic of Korea (PROK)
4. The Salvation Army
5. The Anglican Church
6. Evangelical Church in Korea (An indigenous body)

Total membership of the above denominations approximates 3 million; other Protestant denominations approximate another 5 million Christians.

PROGRAM STRUCTURE

The Council functions through seven standing committees, eight special committees and four sub-committees. Examples of standing committees are Mission in Evangelism and Church in Society. Special committees include Human Rights and International Affairs.

PRESENT OFFICERS

Chairperson:	Rev. Cho, Yong Sool (Evangelical Church)
Vice Chairperson	Rev. Park, Chi Soon (PCK)
Secretary	Rev. Cho, Seung Heuk (Methodist)
Vice-Secretary	Capt. Kim, Chong Wun (Salvation Army)
Treasurer	Rev. Kim, Sang Keun (PROK)
General Secretary	Rev. Dr. Kim, So Young (PCK)

STUDY ACTION GUIDE

I. WHY KOREA?

The Program Committee on Education for Mission of the National Council of Churches of Christ in the U.S.A. set the framework for the geographical study for 1984-85 by choosing Korea. Why Korea?

In 1984-85 the Korean Protestant community will celebrate 100 years of life and witness in that country. The churches of Korea are laying careful plans for this observance and are inviting the churches of North America to share in the celebration.

The rapid growth of Christian churches in Korea during the past century is the most remarkable growth in Asia. Presently there are about six million Christians in Korea. Even with that history, part of the celebration observance is a 10-year evangelistic program with a goal of doubling the membership of the church in 1985.

Strong evidence exists of a vigorous life within the Korean church — a dynamic approach to rural and urban evangelism, a biblical orientation, piety and prayerfulness, a sense of world mission (93 Korean missionaries sent to 26 countries), creative use of mass media, health agencies, educational institutions, women's involvement and youth programs.

At the same time, the Korean church has been identified closely with national life. Korean Christians were among those resisting Japan's colonial occupation from 1905 to 1945 and were later victims of the Korean war. Out of their sense of mission, they led the anti-communist democratic forces thereafter and are currently leading the anti-dictatorial democratic forces. Many Korean Christians have suffered and are suffering greatly for their beliefs. In these areas of mission, within its own country, the Korean church stands as a model for mission. The dramatic stories of their hopes and purposeful sufferings are worth recounting.

Other factors make it important for North American Christians to be concerned about Korea: the geographic proximity of the Korean peninsula to the Communist powers of China and the Soviet Union and the economic power of Japan; the military support to the Republic of Korea from the United States; the growing trade relationship between Korea and both Canada and the United States.

North Americans have been closely linked with Koreans, both in their Christian experience and in their national life, during the last century. In that time period, the U.S. authorities accepted the dominance of the Japanese empire over Korea, later — without consulting the Koreans — divided the country with the Soviet Union and then fought a war for the southern half of the country. Since World War II, and up to the present, the United States has invested heavily in the Korean economic growth and military forces. It has continued that support for the military government which has taken over the political leadership.

The Korean Christian churches' response to this 100 years of history makes it a case study for mission from which North American churches could learn.

A further element has developed in recent years which makes Korea of specific interest to American Christians — that is the coming of Korean Christians to the United States. At the present time they are the fastest growing element of many North American denominations.

Objectives of the Study

1. To examine the development of the Korean church.
2. To gain some understanding of the Korean churches theological perspectives.
3. To examine the variety of responses by Korean churches to their societal situation and relate it to the response of North American churches to similar local and global situations.
4. To examine the Korean example of maintaining a healthy balance between word and deed, proclamation and service, evangelism and action for justice.
5. To encourage growth in ecumenical sharing between North American and Korean churches.
6. To appreciate the cultural and historical heritage of Korean-Americans.
7. To understand the current situation of the Christian community in Korea.
8. To indicate the ambiguity of the impact the United States and Canada have had on Korea.

Resources for the Study are:

1. Basic Study Book: *Fire Beneath the Frost* by Peggy Billings
2. Companion Books:
   Song of the Soul: In Celebration of Korea by Lenore Beecham

The Wish: Poems of Contemporary Korea Edited by Lee Sun-ai and Don Luce

Caring, Growing Changing: A History of the Protestant Mission in Korea by Martha Huntley

3. *Map 'n' Photos: Korea*
4. Children's Books:

Won Gil's Secret Diary (Grades 1-3) by Ruth Cook Burkholder

Mi Jun's Difficult Decision (Grades 4-6) by Ruth Cook Burkholder

Exploring Korea, A Guide to Teaching "Won Gil's Secret Diary" and "Mi Jun's Difficult Decision" by Ruth Cook Burkholder and Carrie Lou Goddard

5. Filmstrip: *In Hope, Witnessing* by Friendship Press

II. PURPOSE OF THE BASIC BOOK

The purpose of the basic book is to help the reader and those using it for study to understand how Korean Christians have grappled with the implications of the gospel in their context. Korean churches continue to be caught up in the political and socio-economic struggles of their nation which began in the earliest days of the church. This involvement has been expressed in acts of individual courage and in a variety of institutional actions. The text has been written largely by Koreans and all the material has been prepared from their perspective.

From the outset it is important to state that the text is written from a particular point of view. It draws heavily on the knowledge, experience and theological understanding of those Christians who are active in the current democratic struggle and who have suffered greatly for their beliefs. Their sense of mission and their views are the dominant views expressed here. This understanding of mission has called for work among Korea's poorest people: the factory workers, poor farmers and alienated young people. It has produced a theology born out of the experience of suffering. At first, the experience was second-hand, as the churches struggled to understand what poor people faced. It became first-hand as they themselves began to be arrested, misunderstood and criticized by the government and other sectors of the public. The result is a theology of the "marginalized ones."

Characterized by its ecumenical and international nature, this sense of mission was born on the factory floors, on oppressed campuses, in the sweatshops of the Seoul Peace Market and on the farms of rural Korea. It was nurtured in prisons and has now reached out to people in all churches and in many countries.

This experience must not be romanticized. It is grounded in reality with all its unpleasantness. This sense of mission in Korea has been rooted in Bible study and maintains a fierce commitment to evangelism and social witness as being one, both to proclaiming the Word and to doing the Word.

It is hoped that Christians in the United States and Canada can relate the learning and insight to their journeys of faith and that mutual strengthening and supportive actions will result.

III. DESIGN FOR THE STUDY

The basic book is designed for use by adult and youth. It is built around four units. Each unit can take from 1 to 3 sessions, depending on the period of time available.

1. Encounter with tradition:

a) to help the reader understand something of the history and culture of Korea, particularly the period of the late Yi dynasty at the turn of the 19th century;

b) to explain the experience — military, diplomatic, religious and mercantile — of Korea with other countries, especially China, Japan, and the United States;

c) to help the reader understand the class structure of Yi dynasty Korea and why Koreans responded so positively to the introduction of Christianity;

d) to establish the division between those who were the society's elite and those who were of lower status and the scholars who identified with each. In order to understand present power relationships, the division will need to be traced from the Yi dynasty;

e) to understand the central role religions, including indigenous religions, have played.

2. Struggles for national independence and for democracy:

a) to gain information on how Koreans feel about freedom and national self-determination by examining such movements as:

— the 1894 Tongkak Rebellion
— the 1919 Sam Il uprising against the Japanese
— the struggle against dictatorships including the 1961 student uprising and subsequent events

b) to examine the role of the church in each period by studying actions they took, the writings and public statements made by Christian groups, particularly theological statements and letters to the churches abroad.

3. Relations on the international scene:

a) to enable the reader to sense the dynamic of the interplay between the major powers present in this region (China, the Soviet Union, Japan and the U.S.A.) and how Korea was and is the stage upon which some of these struggles for power occurred;

b) to offer facts about Korea's present economic and political situation, with an emphasis on the effects of the continued division into northern and southern Korea, the heavy militarization of the society and the push for rapid industrialization based on an export model. One result has been mass migration from Korea to other countries, including the United States.

4. The role of religion in Korean life:

a) to understand the pervasiveness of native religious thought such as Shamanism, its strengths and weaknesses;

b) to examine the development of Christian institutions and gain understanding of the rapid growth of the churches;

c) to focus on the present period of industrialization and its impact on every aspect of society and the church's response by examining the Urban Industrial Mission (UIM) program of the churches, its definition of mission, its theology and its lesson for churches there and here.

IV. STUDY AIDS

1. Study Questions

Each chapter of the basic book is followed by a series of questions. These questions can be used by the individual reader or can be used by a leader/teacher in a variety of ways in group session. They can be used for:

a) review at the end of a study session;

b) assignments for small group discussions which would then be reported to the larger group;

c) writing projects in conjunction with other resources.

2. Additional Resources and Activities

A list of additional resources and activities follows the unit by unit study suggestions.

3. Related Organizations

This list includes the names of related organizations with specific purposes. They can be contacted for additional information if you decide to go into an area in-depth. Remember to allow 3-4 weeks for an answer.

4. Learning Center

A learning center (one room or a special section of the church library) can be an invaluable study resource. It should contain copies of all the material — both print and audiovisual — suggested for this study, as well as additional material collected from magazines, newspapers and other sources. Posters, maps and photographs also enliven a learning center. Taped messages which could be played on a cassette recorder could be another feature. Remember to include cultural information including copies of the poetry in this book and art objects which local residents or church members might loan to the Learning Center. Work space for individuals and small groups should also be available in the Learning Center.

5. "People" Resources

Korean-Americans or returned missionaries may live near you. They can be invited for firsthand human interest and will make an invaluable contribution. Remember that each person has his/her own perspective. Do not expect all people to agree with each other or with the views expressed in this text. Be especially sensitive to people's political views. However, do not use an individual as a substitute for studying all the relevant material.

6. Action Suggestions

Involvement reinforces the learning of ideas and acquiring of information. It is hoped that understanding of Korea and the Korean church and its faithfulness under stress will empower people here to take actions for justice.

7. Mission History

The book *Caring, Growing, Changing: A History of the Protestant Mission in Korea* would be an informative supplement to use throughout the study. Leaders might plan to have a report on the book from a volunteer as an alternate activity in Session Four: "Christianity in Korea." Or volunteers might report on different chapters throughout the study sessions.

8. *Map 'n' Photos: Korea*

This four-color wall map is a useful resource for several of the sessions. During the first session it can be used to show the proximity of the three major Asian powers and Korea's strategic location. The information printed on the back will help in understanding both the history of Protestant mission work and the current work of Korean churches. The photos show Korean church life today and can supplement the session on "Christianity in Korea."

9. Audiovisual

The filmstrip "In Hope, Witnessing" is an important audiovisual look at the church in Korea. It might be used either to introduce the study or to conclude it. The script gives an overview of church life in Korea and the slides allow viewers to glimpse the people of the church.

V. SUGGESTED STUDY PLAN

Session One:
"Encounter with Tradition or The People of Han"

Objectives:

— To introduce the study
— To gain knowledge of the history and culture of Korea

Preparation:

Read this book, including the guidance portion, thoroughly. Mark any items in the content portion which you believe will be of particular interest to your study group. Plan which activities and extra resources you will want to use. Be sure to order the resources and recruit necessary volunteers for the first session's work far enough in advance of the study to permit thorough preparation. Publicity and planning is of course essential to the success of the study.

After making decisions for the overall plan, reread Chapter I of the content section and review the plans for the study session. As leader, you will want to be ready to introduce the subject, the resources and the study process.

The Session:

1. Introduce the text, the additional resources and explain the use of the Learning Center, if one has been prepared. Use material in the "Introduction" of the content portion by Peggy Billings and in this Study Action Guide Parts I and II.

2. Explain the outline of the study process, using material on the design suggested in this Study Action Guide, Part III, or a modified outline planned by you based on your local situation.

3. Begin by asking each person to reflect on the first time they heard of Korea. Write down on paper your first encounter. (Examples might be: "Watching M.A.S.H.." "My son served in the Korean War." "Wearing NIKE shoes.") Then ask people to discuss what they have written in small groups. Allow about five minutes for this and then share the results in the larger group. Highlight as a group some important and some superficial contact and what was learned through each contact. Tell the group that they will return to some of these examples as the study progresses.

4. Brief lecture by teacher/leader (or another person alerted to prepare in advance) on the content of this chapter/unit. Close by having someone read the poem "The Empty Field" by Kim, Chi Ha.

5. Allow time for discussion and questions for clarification. Review the questions at the end of the chapter. Encourage people to express the emotions they felt as they listened to Kim, Chi Ha's poem.

6. Make assignments for next session. (See "Preparation" section in Session Two.)

7. Close with prayer for the people of Korea.

Session Two:
"Korea and the Powers: The Hare in the Tiger's Den"

Objectives:

— To become aware of the background of the major world powers' relationships with Korea

— To identify the positive and negative features of these relationships

— To understand how Korea's present society has been shaped by foreign relations.

Preparation:

At least one week prior to the study, ask three people to help prepare for it. Give one person the assignment to talk about the relationship of Japan to Korea, another the United States (or Canada) and another, that of China and Russia. In addition to the material in Chapter II of the Billings' book, they should look through the other chapters for references and also use reference books in the church or public library. Consult the Learning Center, too.

It is important in this session to have a map of Korea and the surrounding area for use in the oral reports. A small one is included at the end of this guide. *Map 'n' Photos: Korea* also shows part of the area. The "bridge" role Korea has played through the centuries can be seen clearly in this way.

The poetry book, *The Wish*, is an excellent source for the area reports. Members of the study group should be encouraged to see these poems, many of them anonymous, as accurate examples of Korean feelings. They tend to be more melancholy and bitter than Western poems. Why this is so is a useful question to discuss in this sesssion.

The Session:

1. Begin the session by reviewing the materials on "Folk Customs" in this book. Then read together the folk story which opens Chapter II. Break up into small groups to discuss question 1 at the end of Chapter II.

Also ask this question: "Do you think this folk story can apply to Korea's domestic relationships as well as to its external relationships?" Ask each group to compile a list of their answers.

2. In the total group, share the results of the small group discussions. One way to articulate the learning from this exercise is to have volunteers role-play the folk story. Encourage them to show their imagination in their acting, for Koreans are very dramatic and love to laugh at their many tiger stories. Another exercise would be to ask group members to creat their own versions.

3. Now move to the three area reports:
    a) Korea's relationships with Japan,
    b) Korea's relationships with China and Russia,
    c) Korea's relationships with the U.S. (and/or Canada).

After the reports, divide the group into three groups representing the different areas to share with each other what new information they learned. Ask them to review the other questions at the end of Chapter II.

4. Review and reflection. Using newsprint or the chalk board, make a list of all the ways this country relates to Korea. For example, diplomatic relations, military support, economic aid, business (multi-national corporations), tourism, cultural exchanges, church-to-church relations and missionaries. Share in group prayer by mentioning each relationship and allowing time for silent reflection and a short verbal intercession.

5. As a home assignment, ask each person to draft a letter to an imaginary Korean person, expressing feelings about the learnings out of this session. These letters could be shared in subsequent session if the group desires.

An alternative assignment, or one which can be used for feedback in a future session, would be to ask each person to monitor the local newspaper and TV to see how Korea and other parts of Asia are covered.

6. Make assignments for the next session based on the "Preparation" section of Session Three.

Session Three: "The Role of Major Religions"

Objectives:

— To become informed about the religions which have arisen in Korea and those which have played a major role in its development

— To appreciate the importance of religions in Korean life

— To explore what parallels or similarities our religious experience might have to that of Koreans

Preparation:

As an advance assignment, ask for volunteers to prepare a picture exhibit on the religions covered in Chapter III. (It may not be possible to locate material on all the religions talked about in Chapter III.) Schools, museums and private individuals who have lived or traveled in Asia may be sources. Some travel posters may be useful, if they are not exploitative. Arrange the exhibit in the room you use for study, or in a hallway or lounge nearby.

Ask for volunteers who will take the advance assignment to prepare for a panel discussion on the major religions: Shamanism, Buddhism, Confucianism and Ch'ondogyo. If your church is located in a college town, you may be able to find resource persons on the campus who could provide a panel. Also look in your local directory of religious institutions to see if any Buddhist groups are listed. This would be an excellent time to use outside resource people.

The Session:

1. Review the earlier exercise (Session 1) in which participants were asked to reflect on their first contact with Korea. Have people call out one or two words to recall that experience. Then shift to a recollection of the reflections and intercessory prayers (Session 2) on this country's relationships with Korea. Follow this with a re-reading of one of the poems used so far, choosing one that you sensed made a deep impression. Ask each person to use paper and pencil to note changes or developments in their impressions of Korea. If time permits, you may want to ask two or three people to share these reflections. This would be a good time to ask if anyone wanted to share their letter to an imaginary Korean. The purpose of this exercise is to gauge changes in attitudes, to help people sense if they are moving from superficial knowledge to understanding and to express their feelings about the shifts.

2. Write the major beliefs and practices of each religion on a separate sheet of newsprint and place the sheets around the room so they can be easily seen.

3. Open the panel discussion by using a summary of the first page of Chapter III. Then present the panel. When the panel has concluded, divide into small groups to identify discussion questions, reconvene and raise the questions with the panel.

4. Close the discussion by summarizing. Examples of summary learnings might be:

    . . . Korea has many religious traditions.

    . . . Korea has been a bridge for the transmittal of religions from China and Japan.

    . . . Some of these religions originated in Korea and have unique features because of that.

5. Make assignments for the next session based on the "Preparation" section of Session Four.

Session Four:
"Christianity in Korea"
Objectives:

— To become knowledgeable about the introduction of Christianity into Korea and how the churches started there

— To gain understanding of how the church has been influence by social conditions and how it in turn, has influenced events

— To explore attitudes on the missionary movement and how churches around the world can relate to each other

— To gain insight into the theological currents which have run through the life of the church in Korea and continue into today

— To experience the method of theological reflection called "Social Biography"

Preparation:

1. The use of the material in Chapter IV of the basic book can best be studied if it is done by topics which cut across the chronological material. The group could be divided into four subgroups using the following suggestions for topics:

Subgroup A: How the Korean Church Relates to Society

Assignment: Find out how the church and/or individual Christians have related to the building of the nation. What issues have concerned them through the years? For example, Christians participated in the struggle for independence, including insurrection. They have joined in underground movements. How do you feel about this? What do you think you would do if you lived in Korea? The study should bring out the facts as well as feelings about the issues.

This subgroup should also explore the question: Why has the church grown so quickly in Korea?

Subgroup B: The Role of the Bible

Assignment: Explore the importance given to Bible study. Why was the Bible able to play such a central role? What Bible stories have been favorites? Why? How was the Bible used to influence Christian social action? Read those scriptures aloud in your group. Try to imagine how these scriptures would sound to patriots in the middle of a struggle against a foreign occupying power. How should scripture be used as a guide to behavior and action in society?

Subgroup C: The Role of Missionaries

Assignment: Explore the early Nevius method. What was it? How would you evaluate it as a way of doing mission work? What was the comity agreement worked out for mission work in Korea? What was its purpose? What do you think happened to change the early desire for united work into denominationalism and schism? How have missionary attitudes influenced the struggle of the church in society? How do you feel about the sending of missionaries to other countries? How do you feel about other countries, including Korea, sending missionaries to this country? How can churches around the world best relate to each other?

Subgroup D: Theological Trends in the Korean Church

Assignment: Search through the material in Chapter IV of the basic book for the ideas and arguments in the Korean churches about the nature of the church and what it should do. Where did the theological ideas come from? What is the basic argument? What changes are taking place? What is "minjung" theology? Even though it is a minority voice, why is it important? Test out the method of social biography by thinking of how you could translate it into your own experience. Whose story would you tell?

2. Have each group report back to the whole group. Allow time for questions and discussion.

3. Close by singing the hymn from *Song of the Soul: In Celebration of Korea* or another well-loved hymn and with a period of silent reflection on the church. End with prayer.

4. Make assignments based on the "Preparation" section of Session Five.

Session Five:
"From 'Han' (Suffering) to Joy"
Objectives:

— To illustrate the depths of the common people's suffering in Korea by examining folk songs and folk tales as a basis for Korean theology

— To examine the impact on the church of oppression in the modern era

— To understand the learnings which some Christians have gained from the current church-state struggle by examining what is popularly called "minjung" theology

Preparation:

In advance, ask a few people to prepare to teach the group to sing the folk song "In My Native Village" in *Song of the Soul: In Celebration of Korea*, or "Arrirang" in this book, and to read some modern poems either from this book or from *The Wish* and to tell some of the folk stories, including the stories in Chapter III (Billings book). Choose songs and stories which illustrate both melancholy and humor.

The Session:

1. Open the session with a period of singing, poetry reading and story-telling.

2. For a period of Bible study, have the group work in pairs on this assignment: "See how many examples you can find of Jesus using stories to get across his message. List some of your favorite stories. List some of the ordinary things Jesus talked about. Who listened to Jesus?"

Return to the whole group to summarize learnings. Jesus' usual method of teaching was by story-telling or parables. He talked about ordinary, but important things in people's lives — lost money (a crisis for poor people), lost farm animals (a crisis for farmers), a man who was robbed and beaten up, a woman who had been sick for many years, a son who had run away from home, young women preparing for a wedding who forgot to get lamp oil. Let the group add other examples and note what the present-day equivalent of these situations might be. Those who listened to Jesus were fishermen, farmers, shepherds, tax collectors, street women. Let the group add to this list, too. It was the common people who "heard him gladly."

3. One of the most striking facts of Korean history is how dissident scholars have made common cause with the most oppressed groups in the society to seek change. Four different examples ar given in Chapter III. Divide the group into four smaller groups to study them. (Use the resource center for other material.)
— Silhak ("Real Learning") movement
— Tonghak ("Eastern Learning") movement
— Early Protestant churches
— "Minjung" theologians of today

4. Assign one person to report back for each group. Others may fill in if the reporter omits an interesting point. Put the comments on newsprint, if time allows, and place the sheets around the room for those who remember facts better if they can see them.

5. The leader closes this session with a presentation of the main points under the question: "What understanding of God have we gained from reading the Bible in the bright light of the people's story?"

6. Follow with the hymn "Once to Every Man and Nation," a reformation hymn which is sung often at KNCC sponsored prayer meetings for human rights and at Galilee Church services.

7. Close with prayer, again allowing time for silent reflection and prayers of intercession for specific situations in the life of Korea and her churches.

ADDITIONAL RESOURCES

(Note to leader: The following are offered to provide opportunities for indepth study and for personal involvement.)

Early in the study will be a good time to encourage those who want to go into more detail to take special assignments which will enrich the balance of the study.

Individuals or task groups could do such things as:

1. Review all the material in the resource center. Point out valuable material which has not yet been used. Locate and add new material.

2. Prepare a poetry reading for the congregation using the book *The Wish* by Lee Sun-ai and Don Luce. The poems in this book could also be included.

3. Plan a cultural evening, using *Song of the Soul: In Celebration of Korea* as a resource. An understanding of the foods, folk stories, art and music of a people is basic to an understanding of the people themselves. If there is a Korean congregation or group in your area, this would be a good opportunity to plan a joint evening of celebration. You may also want to use the filmstrip "In Hope, Witnessing."

4. Research more deeply into one of the educational institutions related to the church in Korea. For example,

write to the International Foundation for Ewha Woman's University, Room 1221, 475 Riverside Drive, New York, NY 10115 for information on Ewha Woman's University, the largest university for women in the world. The office has films, booklets and pamphlets, as well as names and addresses of alumnae who may live in your area. Write to the United Board of Higher Education in Asia, 475 Riverside Drive, Room 1221, New York, NY 10115, for information on other church-related colleges and universities in Korea, such as Yonsei University and Seoul Women's College.

5. Start a human rights study group to develop support for persons and groups in need of support. Write to the North American Coalition on Human Rights in Korea, 110 Maryland Avenue N.E., Washington, D.C. 20002, for up-to-date information, resource material and action suggestions on issue of human rights including economic justice, militarism and U.S.-Korea relations. The Coalition, which is supported by both Canadian and U.S. churches, Protestants and Roman Catholics, can also suggest the names of speakers and resource persons. You may also hear a weekly news update by telephoning the Coalition at 1-202-546- NEWS.

The following *regional groups* relate to the North American Coalition on Human Rights in Korea and could also assist you:
a. Church Committee on Human Rights in Asia, 1821 W. Cullerton Chicago, Il 60608.
b. Committee for a New Korea Policy, 221 Central Avenue, Albany, NY 12206.

6. Another important additional assignment would be to establish a group to study current U.S. and Canadian trade relationships with Korea, and the basis upon which they are built. For example, Canada and the U.S. have been a source of nuclear power development in south Korea. Consult embassies or consulates for material. The following Canadian groups are excellent resources for such a study.
a. GATT-FLY, 11 Madison Avenue, Toronto, Ontario M5R 2S2.
b. Plowshares Monitor, Institute of Peace and Conflict Studies Conrad Brebel College, Waterloo, Ontario, CANADA N2L 3G6.

7. Another subject of great importance is the question of North-South Reunification. You could write to the following groups for information:
a. The United Movement for Democracy and Unification in Korea (UMDUK), 1809 Monroe St., NW, Washington D.C. 20010.
b. The Association of Korean Christian Scholars in North America, Inc., 475 Riverside Drive, Room 1542, New York, NY 10115
c. Also contact local colleges and universities for scholars in this field. You might start in the History Department and Political Science Department.

PHILOSOPHY OF EDUCATION FOR MISSION

Mission is at the heart and center of the Church's life; through the centuries, people of faith have witnessed in word and in deed everywhere on earth. To be the church is to be in mission.

Education for mission enables people to discover the meaning of mission; to learn about the church's involvement throughout the world; to prepare themselves for ministry in mission; and to engage individually and corporately in expressions of mission. Education for mission can be defined as equipping the people of God so that they may widen their vision and invest their strength in meeting opportunities for mission now before them.

MISSION

Mission is obedient response to our Lord and Savior. The risen Christ commissioned his followers to witness to God's love for the world through word and deed. This commission cannot be understood apart from the story of God's action in the world which we find in the scriptures of the Old and New Testaments where we hear the call to live in trust and partnership with God and to participate in the fulfillment of God's purposes in history.

EDUCATION FOR MISSION

Education for mission is necessary because of the tension, incongruity and contradiction which individual Christians and local congregations experience between the gospel proclaimed and the realities of life in the world. Inappropriate ways of dealing with that tension are: to conform; to condemn; to retreat. For people of faith, the only acceptable relationship between the gospel and the world is to live in the midst of the world as ambassadors for Christ; to love the world as God loves it; to serve in the world in such a way as to witness to God's love.

FOR

The middle word of ''education for mission' implies intention and sets the direction. The task is not only to educate *about* mission but to educate toward the clear goal of active participation in God's cause as it is revealed to us in Jesus Christ.

EDUCATION

It is the nature of the community of faith to nurture its members so that they will grow in faith and develop the strength to confront the conflicting experiences of life both within the community and beyond it.

Education sometimes takes place in an individual's encounter with a committed person. It is often a group experience. It always involves relationships—within one's self, between individuals, among people. Thus the leadership style of intentional educational experiences is one of interaction with the participants—teacher and learners being partners in learning.

Education can help people and groups overcome limiting ways and move into more mature expressions of faith. Learning can be said to have taken place when learners are living what they say they believe.

Education is not neutral. It either helps to maintain what is or it enables people to anticipate and live toward new futures for themselves and the world. The latter requires an educational process which integrates awareness, analysis, action and reflection based on the assumption that we learn as we are involved.

USER'S EVALUATION SHEET

Reactions from the users of this guide will be very helpful in planning similar materials in the future. Therefore, we will appreciate your response to the following questions after you have used the guide for your study. After completion, please tear out this page and send it to Editorial Office, Friendship Press, 475 Riverside Drive, Room 772, New York, NY 10115. (Check one square in answer to each question.)

1. In general, I would characterize this guide as:
   _____Very helpful   _____Somewhat helpful   _____Inadequate
   Explain (if possible)_____
   _____

2. In my opinion, the material in this guide related to the age level in my group:
   _____Very well   _____Quite well   _____Inadequately
   Explain_____
   _____

3. The material in the guide coordinated with the study book and theme:
   _____Very well   _____Quite well   _____Inadequately
   Explain_____
   _____

4. Instructions to the leader were:
   _____Easy to follow   _____Sometimes confusing   _____Hard to follow
   Explain_____
   _____

5. The age level of the activities and projects suggested was:
   _____Just right   _____Too high   _____Too low
   Explain_____
   _____

6. The kinds of activities and projects suggested in the study were:
   _____Well coordinated with the theme
   _____Usually appropriate for the study
   _____Not related to the theme as well as they should be
   Explain_____
   _____

In the space provided below please write a short paragraph containing any evaluations or suggestions about the material that you feel would be helpful in planning for future guides of this type.

Setting of guide's use:

Name of Guide_____

I used this guide with_____(age group).

There were _____ individuals in the group.

We had _____ sessions of _____ (time) each.

My denomination_____

Name and address (optional)_____

_____

_____